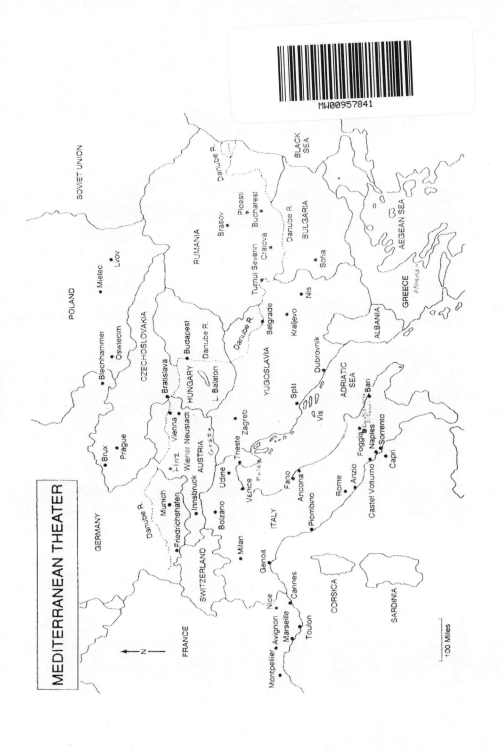

MEDITERRANEAN THEATER

"THE BEST SEAT IN THE HOUSE"

SHORT STORIES AND VIGNETTES

ACHILLES KOZAKIS

To order additional copies of this book, contact:
Xlibris Corporation
1-888-795-4274
www.Xlibris.com
Orders@Xlibris.com
63142

CONTENTS

THE REST OF THE STORIES

SUPPLEMENT 1

SUPPLEMENT 2

PREAMBLE

By
Robert Karstensen, Sr.
President: 451st Bombardment Group (H) Ltd.

The 451st Bombardment Group (H) was called into existence on May 1 1943. On paper it was organized into the 724th, 725th, 726th, 727th Bomb Squadrons, and headquarters section. The first of its Administrative Cadre reported to Davis-Monthan Field, Tucson, Arizona and in June of 1943 was transferred to Dyersburg, Tennessee. Upon completion of organizational duties; assignment of new personnel; and procurement of aircraft, part of the air echelon was sent to Orlando, Florida (Pinecastle Field) for training in the Army Air Forces School of Applied Tactics.

On July 18, 1943 all components of the 451st Bomb Group were shipped to Wendover Field, Utah for the first phases of combat training. Soon Wendover Field was to become too small for the numbers of men that were to maintain the Group. A decision was made to move the Group to larger facilities.

On September 8, 1943 the Group moved to Fairmont Army Air Field, Nebraska, to finalize their overseas training. The 451st maintained high efficiency as they prepared for their Preparation for Overseas Movement (POM) inspection. In mid October the Group passed the requirements of the Inspector General of the War Department and was posted for Overseas Movement.

The Group was under the command of Colonel Robert E.L. Eaton (graduate of the USMA 1931) and was to remain under his command throughout its early combat entity.

The 451st Bomb Group started its overseas deployment in December 1943, flying its aircraft with its crew of 10, plus 4 passengers, using the southern route. This involved stops at Morrison Field, Florida; Borinquen, Puerto Rico (or Waller Field, Trinidad); Atkinson Field, British Guinea; Belem, Brazil; Natal (or Fortalezea), Brazil. From there the Group, in individual flights, jumped-off to North Africa, eventually ending up in Telergma Field, Algeria. A two week layover for the Air Crews in North Africa while the Ground Crews made the base at Gioia Del Colle, Italy adequate to our needs, resulted in extra formation flying and practice bombing missions for those at Telergma Field.

The 451st was to become part of the 15th Army Air Force. It was first assigned to the 47th Bombardment Wing, and later to the 49th Wing, when the decision was made

9

in mid-April to integrate the 461st and 484th Bombardment Groups into the 15th Army Air Force smallest Wing.

Combat flying was initiated on the 30th of January 1944, bombing the Radar Station at Fier, Albania. The Group's first combat loss of men and aircraft occurred on 8th February, When a ship crashed after take-off killing 8 aboard. (Throughout its history the Group was to lose more than 200 aircraft and over 400 of its troops, due to enemy action).

The Group was to gain immortality when, on 25th February 1944, it was to garner its first (of three) Distinguished Unit Citation (DUC) for the bombing of the Regensburg Aircraft Factory in Germany.

The second DUC came as a result of the successful bombing of the Ploesti Oil Installations in Rumania. By this time the Group had moved to its new base in Castelluccio Di Sauri, near Foggia, Italy.

The third DUC came for the efforts in the bombing of the Markersdorf Airdrome, near Vienna, Austria.

All three DUC's were earned while Colonel Eaton had command of the Group. Each was bitterly earned with heavy loss of aircraft and men. Ground crews were called upon to work long and hard hours to keep the Group up to maximum efficiency.

Colonel Eaton relinquished command upon the completion of his 50 prescribed missions to Colonel James B. Knapp. Who, after finishing his required missions, turned command over to Colonel LeRoy L. Stefonowice (A.K.A. Stefen).

The 451st BG flew 245 combat missions from 30th January1944 to 26th April 1945. In September of 1944 the 49th Wing (451st, 461st, and 484th Bomb Groups) flew supply missions of gasoline, bombs and munitions to Lyon, France, aiding the fast moving 3rd Army of General Patton.

The Group showed its diversity in being able to carry out any task assigned. From the bombing of submarine pens, harbor facilities, marshaling yards, air fields, and oil installations to supply runs and pinpoint bombing of bridges in the valleys of Northern Italy, thereby cutting off the retreat of the Germans in their march to regroup. They bombed targets throughout Southern Europe; from France in the East, to Rumania in the West; from Greece in the South, to Poland in the North.

Wherever it was possible for the range of the B-24 to reach, the 451st was there. It was never turned back to flak or fighters. Its determination to reach the target was only deterred by weather conditions, and when radar bombing was perfected, even that became no obstacle to their ability. The Group flew its last mission on the 26th of April 1945 against the marshaling yards at Sachsenburg, Austria. From that time until the end of hostilities, in early May, the Group made arrangements to return all personnel and ships to the United States. In July 1945 it was assigned to Dow Field, Maine, where, on the 26th of September 1945 it was inactivated.

The 451st Bomb Group lives in the minds of all those that served within its ranks. Like the B-24s that served them so well. Soon its personnel will join the ranks of the vanishing aircraft. Like sailing ships of the past, the B-24 and its flight crews; the mechanic and his ingenuity; the armorer and his long hours, will be only a memory to those that will take the time to research our past history.

But for the present the 451st Bomb Group is still a viable entity to many of its former members. It has been reincarnated as a social organization working for the benefit of its loyal following. Its headquarters is not, as its past history has always placed it, at any Army Air Base. Rather it is now located at the home of one of its former air crew members. Robert K. Karstensen, Sr., Marengo, Illinois. It still works for the betterment of its members and within the powers of its office seeks those that once served within its ranks. A proud group still carrying on the tradition of its past—but with no hostilities.

PROLOGUE

The story I am about to unfold should have been told many years ago. Over the past fifty years I have disclosed several of the incidents to my children. In any event, I will attempt to consolidate the past in a chronological manner.

In 1926, Lynn, Massachusetts, a three-year-old boy continuously gasps for a breath of air to "feed" his frail body. The doctor has advised his parents that he doesn't have much of a chance in life. I was that boy!

I do remember, many times, sleeping between my mother and father, when asthma attacks had turned my body blue and my wheezing kept them awake throughout the night. I also remember, during the two years that followed, my father would take me to the doctor for my weekly injections to help overcome and control my asthmatic condition. I guess the reason I remember this so well is that my father would always buy me an ice cream cone because I didn't cry during the doctor's visit.

During these early years of the twenties, my parents, grandparents, Aunt Bessie and Aunt Christina would cautiously protect me from catching a cold. My grandmother crocheted a sleeveless wool sweater that made me itch but kept my chest warm. I wore that sweater for several years.

I was seven years old—almost eight—before I finished the first grade because of my chronic asthma and the date of my birth (October 19, 1923), which made me too young to begin school with children who had earlier birthdays.

As time passed, my asthmatic condition subsided. I'm sure the tender loving care I received and the continuous weekly injections had greatly to do with it.

At eight-and-a-half years old, my mother passed away, a victim of pneumonia, leaving my father with five children: One girl and four boys. My grandparents passed away three years earlier. We were not alone. We had our loving and caring Uncles Theoklis and Charlie, Aunts Bessie and Christina, and cousins, Angie and Little Bessie (Elizabeth) who were more like sisters to me.

The Depression was in full bloom and it was winter with snow on the ground. Ice skating was the sport at that time. My father gathered his four boys, took us to the neighborhood pawn shop and purchased ice skates for all. Mine were three sizes too large, but this didn't stop me from using them! Stuffing newspapers into the toes filled out the skates well enough.

I grew into my skates during the following three winters. I also built up my lungs, chest and legs. I'm certain the continuous exercise was a major factor for outgrowing my asthmatic condition. No longer was I a sickly runt of a kid, but a young lad ready for a fight. And fight I did! With a name like Achilles, I was no pushover, and every boy on the block knew it.

It was a continuous battle, proving to others I was not handicapped because of my childhood illness. I played harder, longer and excelled in all sports for all seasons.

In swimming, I was one of the best swimmers and the youngest Red Cross swimming instructors in Lynn. In football, basketball and soccer, I lettered in high school during my Junior and Senior years. Ice hockey and skiing

were my favorite sports.

In my senior year of high school, on January 30, 1943, I received my "Greetings," (order to report for induction) from the President of the United States. Reporting to the Local Draft Board No. 91 for my physical followed, and to my dismay I was classified 4F, "unfit for military service." I would not believe the results of my physical examination. I was in great shape, no fat, just muscles (lean and mean). I was frustrated and determined to serve in the Army Air Corps. The results of the examination were directly related to my past asthmatic condition and the present sinusitis that was bothering me.

My father was pleased. He felt his two sons, Nick and John, in the service from one family was enough American involvement. The war was in its second year, and I was determined to get involved too.

During my senior year in high school, I joined the Civil Air Patrol (C.A.P.) observing flying aircraft in our area and identifying type and direction of flight. Even though I would spend my Saturdays at the C.A.P. headquarters, I wanted to do more for the war effort and felt my time would be spent more usefully elsewhere.

In a short period of three months that followed, I joined the Coast Guard Auxiliary. There, we were trained and taught the use of fire arms, just like the regular Coast Guard servicemen. On Wednesdays, we held classes and on weekends we were on guard patrol at the Mystic River Docks of Boston and Chelsea, Massachusetts.

In the meantime, I was reinforcing my determination to get into the fight. On my 20th birthday, unknown to my father, I had the nagging polyps removed from my sinuses and shortly after, I volunteered for the Air Corps Cadet program. I was accepted as a cadet candidate in the Army Air Corps.

Learning of my deceptive actions, my father at first was furious, but deep down in his forgiving heart, Pa gave me his blessings and reluctantly approved.

Because of my previous draft call and 4-F classification, I could not immediately enter the Army Air Corps, but would have to wait for the next draft that followed. On the 17th of January, 1944, I entered the Army Air Corps as a Cadet Candidate along with 221 other Candidates from the New England area.

This particular morning was even colder and more wintry than usual. It was snowing all night and ten inches of snow had already fallen, covering the neighborhood with a blanket of white. It was still snowing when my father awakened me at five A.M. because Stanisloski, another Cadet Candidate, who lived nearby in Riverside, came to join me. Of course, the early morning hours didn't bring smiles and I related to Stan that I would meet him at the Lithuanian Club in Riverside at 8 o'clock. Around 7 A.M. I was ready to leave, after embracing my father I shook hands and said good-bye to my younger brother, Milton, who at that time was a Senior in Classical High School.

Meeting Stan in the Lithuanian Club was a mistake on my part. When I arrived, Stan and the bartender were toasting Stan's departure and from the results they were *all* smiles. Even though I didn't drink alcoholic beverages, they insisted that I have one toast with them. I did, and with that drink, my body was hot and I was ready to weather the snowstorm outdoors. We completed our good-byes and took the first bus to Boston's North Station where we embarked by train to Ft. Devens, Massachusetts.

The Class of 221 Air Corps Cadet Candidates were hustled in one area of the camp. There, we were given our first physical exam, given our shots (inoculations), G.I. clothing, uniforms, haircuts and bedrolls. Within a week, we boarded a troop train for Greensborough, North Carolina, our basic training camp and psychomotor testing for aviation school.

Ten weeks of basic training and bivouac finally were completed and we were awaiting our scores for Cadet Training that would follow. The announcement was sharp and clear that 221 men except 2 would not be allowed to continue Cadet Training. Stanisloski and Thomas, a young man from New Hampshire, were the lucky sons-of-a-gun. They had previous flying records and were accepted.

I later learned that 28,000 men in the Cadet program were being "washed out" simultaneously because they were no longer essential for the war effort.

What happened to the remaining class of 219 men? We were given a choice of service in the U. S. Army—Paratrooper, Infantry, or Aerial Gunner. I chose Aerial Gunnery School because I enlisted to fly and fly I would. I venture to say that 80 percent of the men chose gunnery also.

We boarded our troop train in Greensborough, N.C. and six days later we began gunnery classes at Laredo Air Field located in Laredo, Texas.

Physical training (PT) twice a day was rough on many candidates. To me, it was a snap, because of my physical fitness prior to entering the Army. The instructor allowed me to join the boxing team where I competed with permanent party service men.

Gunnery School, to me, was like a game that I enjoyed. Learning to dismantle, assemble and fire the 30 caliber and 50 caliber machine guns became second nature to me. My previous years of studying air craft of all nations, allowed me to identify aircraft at one hundredth of a second. One of the prerequisites before graduating gunnery school was to assemble a 50 caliber machine gun blindfolded with gloves on and set "head spacing" on the gun.

The last two weeks were spent on the gunnery range. There, we fired shotguns (skeet), 30 caliber and 50 caliber machine guns at moving targets on the ground and in the air.

We also learned to operate and maintain all gun turrets of the B-24 and B-17 heavy bombers.

Graduation day from Gunnery School came on June 20, 1944. We were given our "wings" (badge) and also our personal records, including a 15 day delay en route (furlough) to Westover Field located in the suburbs of Springfield, Massachusetts. How lucky can a guy get? Less than 100 miles from my hometown!! There was a mass exodus from gunnery school that day. The graduates of that particular class were happily on their way home and thence reporting at Westover Field on the 6th of July. Our "Orders Number 52" were to report to the Headquarters Section "E"—Trainee (RTU Combat Crews) 112th AAF Base Unit (Bomb (H) AAB, Westover Field, Massachusetts."

On my routing to Lynn, Massachusetts (my home town), I spent two days with my youngest brother, Milton, who was stationed at Scott Field, St. Louis, Missouri, as a student for aerial radio operator.

The next 90 days were hectic and time consuming. Our flight crews were formed. We flew together, lived together, and learned to respect and depend on each other. We flew mornings, afternoons, and nights; a different type of mission each time we flew: Gunnery and Bombardier training off of Montauk Point, Long Island, camera gunnery (tracking and shooting P-47's), simulating fighter attacks and navigational training within the New England area. We practiced formation flying, giving the pilot and co-pilot experience before flying into combat.

By mid-September, we completed our transitional training and reported to the Commanding Offices at Langley Field, Virginia, where we were issued our aircraft, a B-24J "Liberator" Heavy Bomber. There, we practiced flying day and night getting accustomed to "our" new aircraft, Serial Number 42-51993, and we named it "Pat's Wagon" after Lt. Harold S. Patterson, our beloved pilot.

Within two weeks we began our trip to European Theater of Operation (ETO) via Grenier Field, New Hampshire; Gander Lake, New Foundland; Azores, Mid Atlantic Ocean; Marrakesh, Morocco; Tunis, Tunisia, and finally Naples, Italy.

The stories and vignettes shall reveal the life of air combat crews and ground crews of the 451st Bombardment Group (H) in the 15th Air Force stationed in Southern Italy.

I must tell you, I began writing this book 17 years ago when I learned of the recent younger generations that followed mine were not aware of the daily life of air and ground crews. I am writing this book for my children, grandchildren and for others that follow. In time, we shall not be around to tell our stories; I hope they will appreciate and remember why it was the right thing to do.

PREFACE

The short stories and vignettes are the basic elements of "The Best Seat in the House." This book has been underway intermittently for 17 years. The actions of me, my crew, squadron and group were from my recollections, data from my personal combat flying records, my mission log, and notes taken from historical records.

Living conditions existing at the time I was there (1944-1945) may vary from one bomb group to another. The 451st Bombardment Group (H) was located on the Foggia Plain, on an existing wheat field converted to a heavy bomber air base. Castelluccio Dei Sauri, a village of over 600 inhabitants, located approximately three kilometers from Group Headquarters provided local personnel such as laborers, mess hall attendants, laundry, and other functions deemed necessary to keep the base functioning.

Our prime targets were oil related, i.e., oil refineries, petrochemical plants, manufacturing plants for aircraft, tanks and trucks. These targets were bombed continuously to deprive Nazi Germany of its war waging capabilities.

Marshalling Yards (rail and rolling stock) in major cities of supply and check points we hit continuously throughout the bombing campaign to deny the enemy of their critical supply of reinforcements and materials. They repair them; we bomb them (a continuous cat and mouse game)!

During the late months of the bombing campaign, bridges and enemy troop concentrations were on our list of targets as many groups became a tactical force when strategic targets diminished because of the Allies' advances.

Many missions during the months of August and September, 1944, were supply missions for Gen. Patch's American Seventh Army and Gen. Patton's Third Army in Southern France. During the month of April, 1945, the 451st Bombardment Group and several other groups ferried American Prisoners of War from liberated Rumania and Hungary to Bari, Italy; freedom at last for those P.O.W.'s!

I visited our Base Headquarters and neighboring Castelluccio Dei Sauri on two occasions: Oct. 1997 and again Oct. 1999. The airfield (runway and revetments were plowed over and the original wheat fields have been restored. The buildings that remain are located at Group Headquarters Area, the residence of a Rear Admiral of the Italian Navy, and one building at the 727th Squadron area, where a mother and her son live in one end of the building and the livestock in the other end. The olive and almond groves around the 724th Squadron remain and still produce fruit and nuts.

Today, Castelluccio (as we called it) is a thriving city and not a village, completely rebuilt with a main boulevard leading into the city center from the connecting highway.

The streets are paved and ample room for two-way traffic exists. (Not the donkey cart driveways of the past). The Central Square houses the Municipal Buildings where shops and restaurants abound in the area.

I met Mr. Paolo DeFluemeri, who, at 15 years of age, worked in the 727th mess hall. I'm sure our presence during the war assisted many families to survive during the bleak years. Paolo and I walked the air base areas as he described the changes that followed after the 451st departed.

There comes a time in a man's life when he thinks, is this the beginning or the end? I ponder my actions and reactions during my tour of duty. Many times I experienced the site of death and the will to live. Many of my buddies and other young men died too soon. They knew more about death than they knew about life. I think of the men, with joy, that completed their tours and in the same moment I think of the crews that were shot down, their bodies that have never been found strewn in the forests and fields. These men richly deserve our thanks and recognition for their deeds—and their ultimate sacrifice. I sincerely believe that I completed my tour because of my crewmen and my pilot's skill and cool-headedness in combat under severely stressful conditions.

During the month of July, 1945, the crew I loved, which trained and flew combat missions together for the duration of the war, was dissolved and each member reassigned, which brought a void in my life. The bond we forged during the stress of combat lasts a lifetime. Today I am 87 years old and I am the lone survivor of my beloved crew. The bond remains within me.

This book is dedicated to the memory of the crew[*], all great brave men, heroes, and dedicated beyond the call of duty. You are all sorely missed:

---

[*]   H. S. Patterson's Crew: A replacement crew, Oct., 1944 and later, Jan., 1945, became the Lead Crew of Flight "B" of the 726th Bomb Squadron, 451st Bombardment Group, 49th Bomb Wing, 15th Air Force, (USAAF).

Shipment No. FW-	-AY-9	Project No. 90802-R	APO No. 16435-AY-9
B-24J	Crew No. FW- -AY-9		#42-51993

1st Lt.	Patterson, Harold S.	0715309	(P)	Pilot
2nd Lt.	Thurman, Thomas L.	0832285	(CP)	Co-Pilot
1st Lt.	Schilling, Burton	02062617	(N)	Navigator
T/Sgt.	Realley, George W., Jr.	33600362	(E)	Engineer
T/Sgt.	Carrington, Walter A.	11101309	(RO)	Radio Operator
S/Sgt.	Balzer, Lauren A.	19201417	(BG)	Ball Gunner
S/Sgt.	Kozakis, Achilles	31430427	(NG)	Nose Gunner
S/Sgt.	O'Laughlin, Walter E.	16018752	(WG)	Waist Gunner
S/Sgt.	Rodriguez, Demetrio P., Jr.	39862762	(TG)	Tail Gunner
1st. Lt.	Bodie, William E. "Dead Eye"	(B)		Bombardier
2nd. Lt.	Hardesty, Malcolm W.	(B)		Bombardier

The aforementioned bombardiers became members with our original crew after our arrival to the 726th squadron.

ACKNOWLEDGEMENTS

SPECIAL THANKS TO a number of people who have assisted me in preparing and writing this book.

My daughter, Anna Marie Carlson and son-in-law, Dr. Don Carlson encouraged me to write the book and with the help of my dear, adopted daughter, Paula Hughes, completed the final editing of this book.

My son, Thomas typed the stories and vignettes as they were completed.

Bob Karstensen, President of the 451st Bombardment Group (H), WWII, Ltd. And publisher of the 451 Ad-Lib magazine for specific information and details of certain missions contained herein.

My wonderful Rena, who read my stories aloud and put up with my corrections.

Diane Joffrion typed many of my stories.

Garcia for read and encouraged me to write more stories.

HEADQUARTERS, GRENIER FIELD
1377 AAF BASE UNIT (NAD, ATC)
MANCHESTER, NEW HAMPSHIRE

OPERATIONS ORDERS)
              :
NO........... 57)

E X T R A C T

SECRET
AUTH: CO GF

10-2-44

/t/

2 October 1944

** ** ** ** **

3. The following named crews WP by air in the aircraft as indicated below at the proper time from Grenier Field, Manchester, New Hampshire, via the North Atlantic Route to Naples, Italy, reporting upon arrival thereat to the Commanding Officer, 19th Replacement Battalion, Naples, Italy, for further assignment and duty with the 15th Air Force.

Shipment No. FW- -AY-9   Project No. 90802-R   APO No. 16435-AY-9
         B-24J   Crew No. FW- -AY-9   #42-51993

2nd Lt.	PATTERSON, HAROLD S.	0715309	(P)
2nd Lt.	THURMAN, THOMAS L.	0832285	(CP)
2nd Lt.	SCHILLING, BURTON	02062617	(N)
Cpl.	Realley, George W., Jr.	33600362	(E)
Cpl.	Carrington, Walter A.	11101309	(RO)
Cpl.	Balzer, Lauren A.	19201417	(AG)
Cpl.	Kozakis, Achilles	31430427	(CG)
S/Sgt.	O'Laughlin, Walter E.	16018752	(CG)
Cpl.	Rodriguez, Demetrio P., Jr.	39862762	(CG)

Shipment No. FW- -AY-2   Project No. 90802-R   APO No. 16435-AY-2
         B-24J   Crew No. FW- -AY-2   -42-51979

1st Lt.	KORTAN, LAVERNE J.	0444155	(P)
2nd Lt.	ENGLE, ALFRED V., JR.	0226369	(CP)
2nd Lt.	CONSTANDY, PETER C.	02060246	(N)
Cpl.	Bowles, James H.	34637295	(E)
Cpl.	Kubacka, Andrew F.	33570843	(RO)
Cpl.	Stevenson, James A.	32834540	(AG)
Cpl.	Taylor, Robert M.	35771559	(CG)
Cpl.	Garver, Jack E.	17098610	(CG)
Cpl.	Potter, William C.	33898376	(CG)

Shipment No. FW- -AY-10   Project No. 90802-R   APO No. 16435-AY-10
         B-24J   Crew No. FW- -AY-10   #42-52011

2nd Lt.	SODERSTROM, EDWARD C.	0715824	(P)
2nd Lt.	FOERHSLER, ROBERT O.	0829609	(CP)
F/O	GOETZ, GEORGE R.	T129142	(N)
Sgt.	Probst, Robert T.	12034513	(E)
Cpl.	DeMarco, Frank A.	32864125	(RO)
Cpl.	Latzke, Kenneth H.	37550080	(AG)
Cpl.	Lonergan, Donald F.	12176341	(CG)
Cpl.	Prescott, Fitzhugh	36672608	(CG)
Cpl.	Tessier, John D.	11086215	(CG)

Note: Two of the above aircraft were lost by enemy action during the first month of our tour of duty. It was later learned, statistically, 35% of the heavy bomber crews completed their tour of duty.

-1-

EXTRACT 3, Operations Orders No. 57, Hqs., Grenier Field, 1377 AAF Base Unit (NAD, ATC), Manchester, N. H. · 2 October 1944   P 2

This is a **PERMANENT** change of station.

Except as may be necessary in the transaction of official business, individuals are prohibited from discussing their oversea destination even by shipment number. They will not file safe arrival telegrams with commercial agencies while enroute and at domestic or oversea destinations.

A flat per diem of seven dollars ($7.00) is authorized for enlisted men for travel and for periods of temporary duty enroute to final destination, in accordance with existing law and regulations, if travel is performed by air. For travel by rail and for periods of delay enroute to final destination, monetary allowance in lieu of rations and quarters is prescribed in accordance with AR-35-4520.

TDN. 501-31 P 431-01-02-03-04-05-07-08 212/50425.

From time of departure from the continental United States until arrival at permanent overseas station, payment of per diem is authorized for a maximum of forty-five (45) days.

The information contained in Paragraphs 26 and 27 of "Preparation for Oversea Movement for AAF Replacement Combat Crews", dtd 1 April 1944, constitutes an integral part of this order.

AUTH. Letter from CG, AAF to CG, ATC, Sub: "Assignment and Reassignment of Military Personnel of the AAF", 12/1/42 and 1st Ind from CG, ATC, to CG, NAW, 12/10/42 and AR 55-120 Par. 3b(2) 19-5; NAW, ATC, by 1st Ind dtd 15 April 1944 to ltr CG, ATC, dtd 7 February 1944. Par 5, SO 267, dtd 26 September 1944 and Par 7, SO 236, dtd 29 September 1944, fr Langley Field, Va.

**   **   **   **   **

By Order of Col. MOORE

J. E. SANDOW
Lt. Col., AC
Director of Operations

OFFICIAL:
KENNETH LIBBY
W.O. (jg) USA
Ass't Operations Officer

THE BEST SEAT IN THE HOUSE

"This is a PERMANENT change of station."

Flying out of Naples, our first landing in Italy, with our crew and with all our rations and worldly possessions intact and tucked snuggly throughout our brand new aircraft, "Pat's Wagon," we headed southeast along the boot of Italy to another air base on the Adriatic coast, South of Bari.

Moments after takeoff and below my No. 1 & No. 2 engines I could readily see gray smoke billow from the belly of Mt. Vesuvius and the village of Pompeii spread out below. Red tile roofs and white stucco buildings, like red & white jelly beans, sprinkled in the fields of contrasting brown to black farm lands recently plowed-over after this fall's harvest. Forest green hills encircled the stoical area.

From my vantage point, "the best seat in the house," within my nose turret and appointed gun position for the duration of my tour of combat duty, I visualize and contemplate the catastrophe that befell the citizens of Pompeii by the eruptions of this now peaceful and serene looking Mt Vesuvius.

Within minutes we are flying over the beautiful Amalfi coast heading southeast. Below, winding, twisting roads are hugging the walls of the terrain, the black, rocky coast extending its fingers out and into the Bay of Naples. It converges with the oncoming tide as waves explode with white foam and specks of sandy coves and beaches splatter the coastline. Off to and below my No. 3 and 4 engines, I savor the sight of light blue-green waters surrounding the Isle of Capri. Little did I know then, that some day in the not-too-distant future, I would return to this restful and peaceful Isle as a tourist at Uncle Sam's expense, when I visit Capri as a "Rest Camp" (I'm getting ahead of myself, that's another story).

Salerno lies just below my left wing and I am soberly reminded of the recent bloody landings of the American 5th Army, notably the 3rd, 36th and 45th Infantry Divisions. Spread above and throughout the cliffs, hills & mountains adjacent to the beaches, the remains of devastated German gun fortifications lie and I visualize the havoc & horror that fell upon brave troops on the beaches below. Have you every looked up into the barrel of a German 88mm artillery piece? That's the feeling I get when I observe the immediate area. The hum of our engines awakens my instinctive reflection and I no longer feel like a tourist nor do I see the beauty passing below.

Minutes have passed and we turn east, the Gulf of Salerno coast is behind us and the mountains and valleys are below and ahead. Soon thereafter we are on our downwind leg of our landing pattern. I scramble out of my turret, secure it, and take my position for landing—at the bomb bay catwalk located just aft and below the command deck.

I crack the bomb bay doors and stand by the generator located below the command deck and to the left of the nose wheel. As our landing wheels hit the steel mat runway, we land with a roar, like a steam locomotive speeding down the tracks. Within minutes we're taxiing and as we do, I start the generator providing electrical power for the aircraft. A jeep with a "follow me" sign guides Pat, our pilot, to a designated revetment and parks the aircraft. San Pancrazio, the home base of the 376th Bomb Group, is an airbase located on the heel of the boot of Italy, a small village between Manduria and Lecce. We bivouac for the night, sleeping on the ground in our sleeping bags. I rise with the morning sunrise, a new beginning. It's my 21st birthday. Wow, what a day!! Breakfast follows and so does another flight northwest to Gioia de Colle.

We anticipated a four hour pass after landing to see the city. However, the Army had other plans for our crew and aircraft. We were hustled into a briefing room and there we learned our aircraft "Pat's Wagon" was to be taken from us and given to some other Bomb Group as a replacement aircraft. Learning of this felt like some monster had plunged into my gut and had devoured my insides. I felt completely empty and highly peeved! Pat tried to condole us, but without much success.

The same evening we again picked up our rations, flying gear and personal possessions and headed for the runway. There, a B-24H, battered and war weary, flew our crew and everything we could carry to our final destination known as the 726th Bomb Squadron of the 451st Bomb Group, 29th Bomb Wing, 15th Air Force, APO 520 (Permanent Change of Station).

It was dark, the night was upon us and the wet, cold air filled the aircraft. There was no joy or joking around, mostly cussing and talking about why our aircraft was taken away. We were just like a bunch of kids after losing a ball game. Pat summed it up and cooled our tempers by explaining how the Army, in its mysterious ways, accomplishes its missions.

The flight from Gioia Del Colli to Castelluccio, our new base, lasted about an hour. Again we hustled out of the taxi aircraft, hopped on a truck with everything we possessed in the world. It took us to the motor pool area of the Squadron.

Everything ran like a typical Army Standard Operational Procedure, *SNAFU*. There was no place to billet us for the night except a tent full of oil drums. Now I know why we had two weeks of bivouac during basic training. This was it!!

I found a dry area with oil drums stacked next to one another like peas in a pod. Grudgingly, I spread my sleeping bag over the oil drums, laid my pooped-out body with a weary mind over the sleeping bag and tried to forget the miserable experience we had this day. Finally, sleep came and the morning followed.

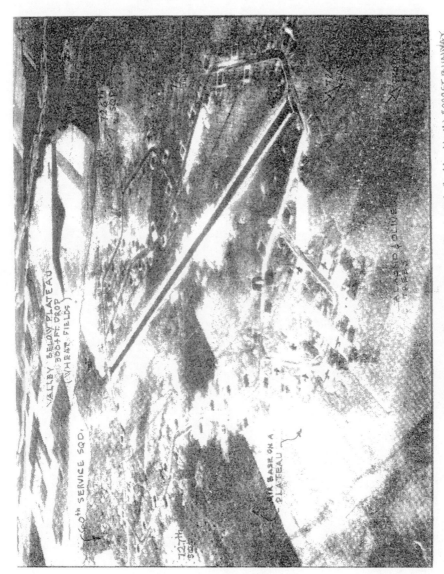

451ST (H) Bombardment Group. Airfield, Castelluccio, Italy (looking North). 5,000 FT. RUNWAY

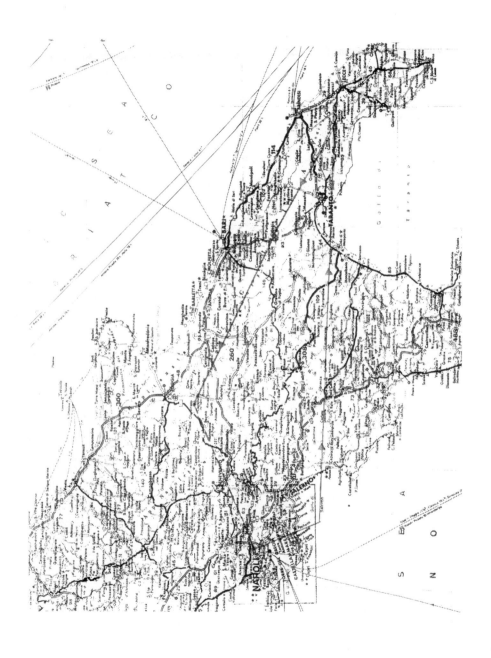

THIRSTY

Arriving at our "Permanent Change of Station" was no picnic. I had hoped this morning would bring a warm reception. Wrong! This is the Army and we are members of a REPLACEMENT CREW, usually treated like the stepchildren of a large family.

Captain Henry B. Ford, Operations Officer, greets us with a smile and tells us how pleased he is to have us on board. I'm sure he is wondering, will this crew live up to the Squadron's high standards of combat flying. After a five minute greeting (speech), we are told to report to the Supply Sergeant. "You can pitch your tent anywhere you please in the enlisted men's area," the Sergeant directs us. There we are issued a tent, a cot, a mattress cover, two blankets and a steel helmet for each crewmember.* The officers of the crew have a tent ready for their move-in at the officers section of the squadron.

Our squadron is located on a plateau about three hundred plus feet overlooking the wheat fields in the valley below. Looking at the squadron enlisted men's area reminds me of a nomadic habitat with tents sprawled like ant mounds on a barren field. No trees, no bushes or vegetation, just black earth enveloping the tent area. Kalichi (sandstone) pathways meander towards the Mess Hall and Squadron Headquarters buildings made of concrete blocks and corrugated roofs. They are the main and most important destinations of the squadron.

"Man," I tell my crewmates with a sigh, "this is home sweet home for the duration."

"Nothing great to write home about," Balzer replies.

We decide to pitch our tent on a remote hilled section encircled with a small grass mat located at the edge of the enlisted men's area. Shortly thereafter, we learn to our dismay why locating in this area was a BIG mistake.

More often than not, some crews, when completing their tour of duty (35 missions), would buzz the squadron at approximately 50 feet above ground level creating a huge prop wash that would shake our tent from its stakes, and the roar of the aircraft engines would scare the hell out of us.

---

* A 16 ft. x 16 ft. tent housed 6 enlisted crewmen, and provided enough space along the tent sides to accommodate 6 cots end to end (two cots per side). The space at the center part of our tent was allocated for a stove, a jerry can for hot water storage, and a small stand to hold our helmets for washing. We had none of the above except for our helmets. Did I mention the floor of our tent? Oh yes, it is Mother Earth!

The back side of the hilled section was located at the edge of a 300 foot drop to the valley below where the buzzing aircraft and its crew would travel just above the valley floor, then a steep climb would ensue and end just above our tent.

We all concurred it was time to move elsewhere. After reviewing the advantages and disadvantages for our tent location, we decide to move next to two aircrew tents and approximately 50 yards from the Mess Hall where the surrounding area had a six-inch fill of Calichi. The Calichi makes a mud free area when it rains.

Sleeping on a cot with no air mattress is impossible to endure. Air mattresses are supposed to be issued to the flight crews. None were available upon our arrival. I just had to do something drastic about this dilemma.

The October chill and the on-coming winter tells us we desperately need a stove to heat our tent and hot water for bathing. The canvas flaps at the entrance of our tent are not draft proof and the night chill enters at will.

"It's time for action and time for moonlight requisitioning or anything that will fulfill our needs," I goad my crewmates. "Let's find the person or persons who can furnish our requirements."

Realley answers, "We can't go around and steal from our squadron!"

"Hell," I respond. "I didn't say steal, I meant we find somebody who can provide our necessities!"

Balzer and O'Laughlin, with his heavy Irish brogue, respond, "We don't know anybody."

Walking over to their side of the tent, I quietly answer with firmness, "get off your asses and go out there, be friendly and ask questions, find, barter, and purchase or bribe someone for our needs."

A day or two pass, and during that time we learn that all our needs can be found at the 60th Service Squadron located approximately one-half mile from our area, and the name most frequently mentioned was "Thirsty."

"Who in hell is Thirsty?" I question my crewmates.

"He is Corporal Thirsty stationed at the 60th Service Squadron," Carrington quips with a grin.

"Thirsty," I repeat. "Man, with a name like that, he most likely drinks a bit."

Rodriguez, our tail gunner, follows with, "I have been told he can requisition anything that is not bolted down or anchored."

The following morning, I take a fifth of Calvert's blended whiskey from my "bag of goodies" and tuck it inside my field jacket as I trudge off to the 60th Service Squadron to find Corporal Thirsty.

My "bag of goodies" contained four fifths of blended whiskey (Calvert's, Three Feathers, and Seagram's Five Crown) that were purchased at the stateside liquor stores. The better grades of whiskey were drafted to the Military Services. One fifth of Canadian Club, one of the better brands of whiskey at that time, cost ninety cents per bottle—one bottle per person. I purchased it in Gander, Newfoundland.

I purchased one bottle of Champagne when we landed in the Azores en route to our "Permanent Station." I planned that we would drink it when we completed our tour of duty.

I didn't drink alcoholic beverages. However, being "street smart," I knew in time, the booze would help me succeed when requisitioning my needs. Now is the day to put the booze to work!

As I approach the 60th Service Squadron, windows and man doors are visible at each house. There are also aircraft-droppable fuel tanks supported on wooden frames made with 2X4's. The tanks are filled with water, and piping with hoses that are connected to an indoor shower. WOW!!

Man, these guys live in high cotton. I know I'm in the right area.

The house I approached had two wooden steps leading up to a massive front door.

I knock loudly and repeatedly. I was sure anybody inside could easily hear me.

Within a minute or so, a tall unshaved buck sergeant curiously opens the door and with an inquisitive gruff voice asks, "What the hell do you want?"

"I'm looking for Thirsty. Do you know where I can find him?" I shoot back.

A few seconds pass while he scrutinizes this young, fuzzy-faced corporal wanting to see Thirsty.

Gruffly, he replies, "Thirsty lives here. He's sacking out on his bunk."

"Eureka," I say to myself, "I found the bastard!"

I quickly entered the casa, a large room about 20 ft. x 30 ft. with a 10 foot ceiling. The interior had a wooden floor that made a household sound as I walked toward Thirsty's bunk. Three empty bunks, a table with four chairs, and a separate bathroom with two closets completed the interior with a large stove in the center of the room. The bunks had genuine springs and mattresses. Adjacent to each bunk, a four shelf bookcase was installed with an assortment of magazines, *Stars and Stripes*, newspapers and personal effects of each tenant.

One bunk is occupied. I see a motionless body lying on its back, with a fatigue cap covering the eyes and arms crossed behind his head. I'm at the foot of the bed approximately two feet away so as not to be too intrusive.

I politely ask, "Are you Thirsty?"

He doesn't respond immediately. Just lies there without moving and not looking. Finally, he says, "What in hell do you want?"

To make a long story short, I explained my dilemma to him and asked him to provide the following items:

1. A stove with fuel tank and tubing
2. A door for our tent
3. A bunk bed with a top to house my A-3 and B-4 bags

Thirsty removes his cap, his eyes wide open, and sees me standing at the foot of his bunk. I take a good look at him; he takes a longer one at me. He is unshaved and his fatigues are wrinkled and most likely slept in. His boots are relatively clean.

Without rising, just lying there, he says sharply, "What makes you think I can deliver all those items?"

"Thirsty," I respond, "Everyone tells me if you need anything," and I emphasized *anything*, go see Thirsty." Well, here I am," I continued opening my field jacket with the fifth of Calvert's staring him in the face.

Immediately he rose with a burst of energy, his eyes bulging and glued on my bottle, his arms lunging for the whiskey. I quickly step out of his reach, knowing I have the bastard!

At that instant, I remove the bottle from my field jacket and make a gesture as if to hand him the bottle, then stop. Holding the bottle a safe distance away, I repeat my request. I tell him in a soft, convincing voice, "Thirsty, this is *all* yours when you deliver the items."

"Look," I continue, there's more where this came from and you know the aircrews receive a two ounce shot of 100% proof rye whiskey after each mission. I'm sure we can be buddies for the duration."

Thirsty is now sitting up on the edge of his bunk and inviting me to sit with him. I'm a bit apprehensive and I tightly hold my bottle while he praises his procurement abilities. Twenty-to-thirty minutes elapse. During that time, we learn a lot about each other and he just can't look away from the Calvert's. I encourage him to make the deal and deliver our requested items within four-to-five days.

In a deep gasp of air he replies, "OK, Greek (he can't pronounce my name), I'll do it and I'll see you in a few days. I promise."

We shook hands, and I held onto the bottle as he drove me back to my tent in his jeep.

After I explained to my crewmates what had transpired, they were elated. They patted me on my back and shook my hand while promising the world to me.

"Take it easy fellows," I caution, "we haven't received the goods yet."

Four days had come and just about gone, when a jeep stops in front of our tent. With curiosity, we look at each other, and then scramble outdoors to see Thirsty with a jeep full of our requested items. The exhilarating chatter that follows brings out some of the men in the neighboring tents.

Thirsty helps us unload and set up the stove, fuel lines, and fuel tank. He installs the door very efficiently as a tradesman with plenty of experience. Then he installs my precious bunk made from 2X4's and slats of wood from frag bomb crates.

"Thirsty," I shout, "Where are the springs for the bunk?"

"None available, Greek," he quickly responds.

"Well, something is better than nothing," I answer with a strained smile.

At this juncture I hand Thirsty *his* bottle of Calvert's whiskey. He grasps the bottle, holding it tightly in his left hand while shaking my right hand with a long firm grip. I humbly request that he visit us anytime.

"I'll always have a drink for you, Thirsty." I pat him on the back to conclude our farewell.

Thirsty became our buddy and dear friend. The sad part is I didn't remember his full name. I know he was of Italian ancestry; first generation born in the U.S.A. (the same as me except my ancestry is Greek) and his hometown was in New Jersey.

A couple of months later and Thirsty took my mattress cover I slept in and had a mattress made with straw by an old lady from nearby Castelluccio.

That's what I call "service and a dear friend." Oh yes, I always had a shot of rye for him whenever he came to visit.

In retrospect, I often thought about this episode and learned that you make the best of what you have. Circumstances create action, and action creates consequences. We both had what the other badly wanted. It was just a matter of time and effort to reach a win-win result. Life has its consequences and, in this case, its rewards.

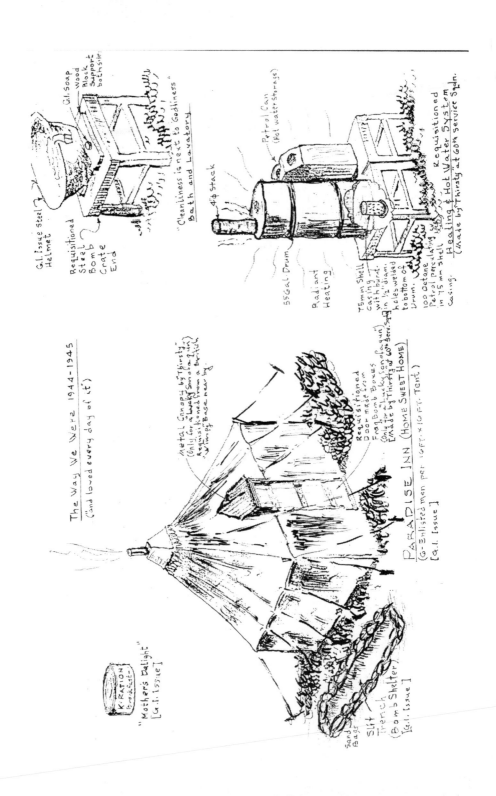

The Way We Were 1944-1945
(and loved every day of it)

G.I. Issue Steel Helmet

G.I. Soap
Wood Block Support - bathside

Requisitioned Steel Bomb Crate End

"Cleanliness is next to Godliness"
Bath and Lavatory

Petrol Can (Hot Water Storage)

4¢ Stack

55 Gal. Drum

Radiant Heating

75mm Shell casing with burnt holes welded to bottom of Drum

100 Octane Petrol percolating in 75 mm Shell Casing.

Requisitioned Hot Water System
Heating & Hot Water System
(Made by Thirsty at 60th Service System)

Metal Canopy by Thirsty
(Only for a lucky few or a 2nd Lt.)
Requisitioned from a British Airways Base near by

Requisitioned Door made from Frag Bomb Boxes
(Only for a lucky Construction)
Made by Thirsty at 60th Service

PARADISE INN (HOME SWEET HOME)
(6 - Enlisted men per 16Ft. x 16 Ft. Tent)
[G.I. Issue]

K-RATION breakfast
"Mothers Delight"
[G.I. Issue]

Slit Trench (Bomb Shelter)
[G.I. Issue]

Sand Bags

"726th STAFF OFFICERS"
L to R: H.B. Ford; R.J. Whiting; J. Reichenbach; B.J. McKinnis

"OFFICERS ROW"
Home for the 726th Officers

Mess Kit wash racks: 726th Area

Enlisted men's tent area—726th.

H.S. PATTERSON'S CREW

(451ˢᵗ Bomb Group, 726ᵗʰ Bomb Squadron)
Oct 1944-May 1945

I recall one day we (the crew) were sitting around in our tent and shooting the breeze about our crew. A brief review of that discussion follows:

Harold S. Patterson, Pilot, 28 years old, Franklin, Indiana. Pat was like a big brother to us. A great pilot and person you could lean on. He, being the oldest replacement pilot in the squadron, made our lives safer because he wasn't cocky and didn't make foolish mistakes. When we flew together it was strictly business—everything by the book and when we were on the ground, he would always look out for our well being.

Thomas Thurman (Jug Butt-3), Co-pilot, 27 years old, Crossville, Tennessee. Tom was the appointed Squadron Gunnery Officer. He was notorious for suckering the boys into skeet shooting for money (making wagers). And of course, Tom would always win. His past time included selling clothes (civilian) from his father's haberdashery back in Crossville.

Burton Schilling, Navigator, 21 years old, East Islip, Long Island, NY. The quiet type, Burt was soft spoken and always very serious. His navigation skills were extremely accurate. Always on course and on time, Burt became one of the Squadron's lead navigators.

William E. (Bill) Bodie, Bombardier, 22 years old, Buffalo, NY. Bill was an easy going guy, lots of laughs in the nose of the aircraft. "Dead Eye" was his reputation and call number. Whenever we flew Lead Ship, he most always made a "shack" (bulls eye).

George W. Realley Jr., Flight Engineer & Top Turret Gunner, 21-1/2 years old, Philadelphia, PA. George did his job very well. One time he put out a fire with his bare hands, earning him the Soldier's Medal. George always bragged about the candy bars that were made in Philly. He did have a point—they were delicious!!

Walter A. Carrington, Radio Operator and Waist Gunner, 24 years old, Waterbury, Connecticut. Walt was another quiet type and kept to himself except on pay day. He was always sure to set aside a portion of his pay to gamble at the N.C.O. club. He managed to win most of the time!

Lauren A. Balzer, Armorer & Ball Turret Gunner, 20 years old, Portland, Oregon. Lauren would always "bitch" about the civilian who complained because he (the civilian) had to stand in the bus on his way to and from his defense job (as noted in the weekly magazine *Yank*). Lauren would swap places with this guy in a blink of an eye and without bitching!!

Achilles Kozakis, Nose Turret Gunner. 21 years old. Lynn, Massachusetts. First generation of Greek ancestry, sometimes affectionately known as "Greek." Achilles didn't smoke and he didn't drink. But he loved to listen to music, when—and wherever he could find it, dancing whenever he could find a partner and of course singing. It needs to be noted that Achilles also liked the girls!

Walter E. O'Laughlin, Waist Gunner. 21 years old. Monticello, Illinois. Walter had an Irish brogue as thick as Scottish kilts! O'Laughlin liked to gamble too, but he would almost always lose. He was conscientious when it came to his work and he was a good man to have on your crew.

Demetrio Page Rodriguez, Jr., Tail Turret Gunner. 23 years old. Taos, New Mexico. Page was a good gunner and even better dice player. His game was chasing girls whenever he went to town. But I must add, Page had slim pickings around Foggia.

Quite a crew, huh?? I would say the *Best* in the Squadron.

After flying combat missions for two months (Nov. and Dec. 1944), our crew (Lt. Harold S. Patterson's crew) became Lead Crew Flt. "B", 726th Bomb Squadron, 451st Bomb Group. The German antiaircraft batteries would concentrate their attacks on the lead ship. Hoping to destroy the formation with "the cream of the crop" air crews that have proven themselves to succeed in air combat warfare, and have successfully performed their assigned tasks.

I sincerely believe I completed my tour of duty because of my pilot's skill and his cool hardy actions under the uttermost stress of combat conditions.

REPLACEMENT CREW FW-AY-9, B-24J, #4251993
15TH AIRFORCE, 451st, BOMB GROUP(H), 726th BOMB
SQUADRON

Top Row Left to Right: A. Kozakis, H. S. Patterson, B. Schilling, T. L. Thurman, G. W. Realley, Jr.

Bottom Row Left to Right: W. A. Carrington, D. P. Rodriquez, Jr., L. A. Balzer, W. E. O'Laughlin October, 1944

LEAD CREW FLIGHT 'B'; 15TH AIRFORCE, 451st BOMB GROUP (H), 726th BOMB SQUADRON; FEBRUARY-MAY 1945

Top Row Left to Right: Thurman, Thomas L. (CP); Patterson, Harold S. (P); Bodie, William (B); Schilling, Burton (N); Hardesty, Malcom (B)

Bottom Row Left to Right: Kozakis, Achilles (NG); Rodriquez, Demetrio P., Jr. (TG); O'Laughlin, Walter E. (WG); Balzer, Lauren A. (AG); Realley, George W., Jr. (E); Carrington, Walter A. (RO)

Pat & Tom, their Return
From Cairo, March 1945.

LATRINE ROUTINE

Flashlight in hand I head out for the latrine located on the crest of a slope about 60 yards from the tent area. The trail is hardened by the constant use of GI's before me as it meanders through a forest of tents with their smoke stacks silhouetted in the starlit sky, like rows of pegs on pyramids.

The night is cold, the air crisp and damp. More often than not, a soft breeze with a breath of winter's chill would pass me by. It is 0300 hrs and the only GI's that are about are the ones flying today's mission and support personnel. You can hear the low whispers of a few men while others trudge on silently with their solemn thoughts as they make their way to their destination. Like the stillness engulfing our tent area, no one is jostling about—just modestly walking. When I arrive at the latrine, the expected line forms and the wait follows.

The "four-holer," as we sometimes called it, composed of four wooden barrel halves with a toilet seat bolted on the top side and secured to a wood deck—most likely made from frag bomb boxes.

The early morning mist seeps through the screened area as one exposes himself to the elements surrounding the cubicle. One or two of us may be fortunate enough to requisition a seat that was previously occupied. A warm seat is more inviting than one that has been standing freely during the night.

This is one of the many routines I became accustomed to in short order. No need to gripe about it. They say that "life is no bowl of cherries"!

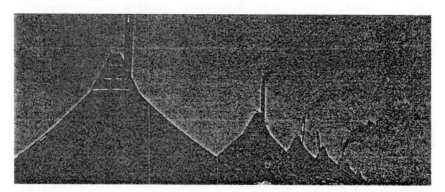

COUNT YOUR BLESSINGS

My crewmate and ball gunner, Lauren Balzer, clomps into the mess hall dressed in his freshly laundered coveralls and wearing his recently polished GI boots, splattered with fresh mud created by this early morning's rain. His mess kit flaring about in all directions, with a disgusted look and with an angry voice, he says, "I wish it would stop raining!" (This is a mild statement compared to the actual words). It was one of those mornings we should have stayed in our tent.

During the winter months in southern Italy, rain is constantly upon us, controlling the paths we take to our destinations. Paths of least resistance through ankle deep Italian black mud are the prime objectives and considerations taken. There are no paths to be had that are covered with stones of any kind or concrete walkways. What little Caliche there was, was reserved for the grounds around the mess hall and operations buildings.

An airbase built on an existing wheat field for the duration gives no mercy to its invading inhabitants. The existing paths crisscross the squadron area like pathways on a New England college campus, or like a spider's web seen through the early morning mist.

During the following night the pouring rain, seemingly endless, again drenched the enlisted men's tent area. The downpour could be heard from within as it bounced off our tent and rolled with a resonating splash into our slit trenches that hugged the tent's perimeter. Thanks to the weather, no air raid alarm bellowed that night!

Morning light broke the darkness. As I peered out onto the field of nature's freshly made sea of mud, I instantly knew I should have stayed in my sack. With a little luck, a tortuous path may be found—one that I could follow and totter on to my destination.

This was not one of our better days!!

Rather than clash with and confront this black quagmire, we forfeited our breakfast and surrendered to the warmth of our bed rolls. Heck, don't feel sorry for these GI's, we were extremely fortunate. The "K" rations were just fine! We were dry and we didn't go hungry, unlike the "dogfaces" feeling miserable in their fox holes with mud up to their ears.

Moral of the story—"You're always better off than you think you are!"

726th Bomb Squadron—Enlisted men's tent area

My personal perception was always that the air crews would die with a
clean shave where as the front line infantry men (dog face) would die
with a dirty shave. A perfect example of this phenomenon is illustrated in
Bill Mauldin's Book titled "Up Front" with the two pitiful, yet loveable
and down to earth. characters, Willie & Joe. In the end, many of us would
survive this conflict and others would not.

WAKE UP CALL

Your name is called.
Deep sleep is shattered.
Immediately, like a Robot
under command you awaken with a start.
You acknowledge the Squadron clerk
who continues to wake the remaining crew
members for this day's mission. It's 0400 hrs
and the tent suddenly becomes alive, like
bees on a hive. Everyone has his routine for
rolling out the sack and dressing. Brief
moments of grumbling and some cussing are
heard and are followed by gestures of
helplessness. Is it the abrupt awakening from
sweet slumber that creates this atmosphere
or is it the day's mission coming upon us?
Maybe it's just a typical GI's "good
morning"?
Within minutes you are fully dressed.
No longer does one hear the grumbling
or cussing, but instead friendly smiles and
salutations. We are after all, a crew, tightly
knit and concerned about each other. Our
goals and agenda are one and the same . . . . to
bring this war to a victorious end as soon as
possible and go home to get on with our
civilian lives.

BEFORE TAKEOFF

The weather briefing officer
tells us it would be C.A.V.U.
over the target area.
It was back to Vienna
again this week!
To strike its refineries
and petrochemical plants
With each passing day
the guns over the target
would multiply.
680 at first and now 800.
Still not enough to stop
our determination.
Crews hustle to their tents
and prepare for the day's mission.
Time is short and take-off time is near.
Each craft has been made ready.
The ground crews toiling
Through-out the night
have done their jobs extremely well.
Engines are being checked
as their roar awakens the morning sun.
The sun's glow clears the mountain tops
and spreads its fingers across
the fields below.
Men & aircraft are ready
for another run.

FLYING THE NOSE TURRET

(Emerson Nose Turret on a B-24 "Liberator", Bomber (H) WWII)

Having the "Best Seat in the House" has its consequences and they say that "seeing is believing." I instantly became a believer—in a big way—during my second mission over Vienna, Austria.

We're flying at 26,000 feet, the weather is C.A.V.U. and I have a great view of what's coming ahead. At 10 o'clock level and at approximately 15-to-20 miles distance, I can see heavy flack and smoking aircraft. My selfish thoughts tell me we're headed for a different target. Wrong! We instantly make a sharp left turn, the initial point of the bomb run (I.P.). Oh my God! We're heading into the same hell I had witness just moments earlier.

I have one thought greater than all others: Will I live? Instantly I begin praying, again and again, "Our Father who art in Heaven . . ." until I gather my wits and strength to overcome my fear. Above all, I cannot let my crew down, and so I continue with my watchful duties.

Bombers flying in a tight formation begin to break up as aircraft, riddled with flak, fall out of formation with smoking engines, some with chunks blown apart. First one, then another, then another, "Oh God, is there no let up?" Aircraft rolling on their backs and falling straight down, I follow them until they're out of my view. I can see no parachutes, only trailing smoke.

There is nothing I can do for my fellows who are being mauled and chopped up by the flak bursting around and on us all. It's so thick—not only can you walk on it, you can smell it too! Scanning our wings, I observe the No. 4 engine knocked out by flak and feathered, leaving us with three engines to straggle home. Momentarily, deep feelings of helplessness and despair overcame me as I watched this unbearable sequence of events.

A far cry from my first mission: A milk run (no flak, no enemy fighters sighted and five hours of flight time) over Sarajevo's marshaling yards—troop concentration. I had no earthly idea how difficult these missions would get.

On the third day following the Vienna mission, the Squadron was bombing an oil refinery in Blechhammer, Germany. Sometimes you think you may get killed, but after a couple of missions it doesn't enter your mind. By this time I had been baptized under fire and my fears, although never completely absent (you never get over it), were somehow weaker, diminished and more controllable. The next mission (fuel dump at Linz, Austria, was called off on way to the target after one hour and 23 minutes of flight time.

Three days of stand downs due to bad weather followed, giving my crewmembers and me a well-deserved rest. But the war goes on and the following five consecutive days (Nov. 16 thru 20, 1944) earned me five more missions, my first Air Medal and Purple Heart. The missions included:

Mission	Pilot
Munich, Germany—Marshalling Yards	Lt. H.S. Patterson
Blechhammer, (South) Germany—Oil Refinery	Lt. F.O. O'Connell
Villa Franco, Italy—Air Drome	Lt. H.S. Patterson
Vienna, Austria—Oil Refinery	Lt. H.S. Patterson
Blechhammer (South) Germany—Oil Refinery	Lt. E.H. Porter

I was told at the end of this memorable month (nine attempts—completing seven missions and/or 12 sorties) that I was now a *"veteran"* and had earned the right to tell war stories and to bitch about them.

P.S. November is my favorite month—I SURVIVED!!

Lt. H.S. Patterson's Crew:
Replacement Crew FW-AY-9 with B-24J, Serial No. 42-51993
H.S. Patterson (P), T.L. Thurman (CP), B. Schilling (N).
A. Kozakis (NG), G.W. Really, Jr. (AEG), W.A. Carrington (ROG).
L.A. Baltazar (BG), W.E. O'Laughlin (WG), D. P Rodriguez (TG)

Blue I was B-24H 41-28853, from the 465th BG, 78Srd BS. She was flown by a mixed crew from the 781st BS. under command of Lt Col C.J. Lokker, as part of the 464th BG formation which attacked image here the south oil refinery at *Blechhamer, Germany*. A direct flak hit in the fuel tanks caused her destruction. Note the bombs spilling out of the bomb bays. Two of the 465th BG's dispatched ships went down on the units 110th mission. flown on *20 November 1944*. A total of 14 B24s from the MTO went down that day. (K. Nelson) My 7th Mission (12 Sorties)

MERRY CHRISTMAS TO ALL

December 24, 1944

The day is wet and cold; the grey clouds hug the mountain tops as the piercing winds blow in from the choppy seas of the Adriatic. Dreary as it is, this time of the year, my thoughts and feelings remind me of my home and family. We would sing Christmas carols and enjoy the days we spent and tied us together. I felt sadness more agonizing during the holidays.

But this is 1944, and although my father and sister with my aunts and uncles and cousins keep the fires burning by working in the defense plants of Lynn, Massachusetts, my brothers and I are far from home taking care of business overseas. My brother John is in the Navy, on submarine patrol in a Corvette, somewhere in the North Atlantic. My oldest brother Nick is stationed in Assam, India. And my youngest brother Milton is a radio operator on a transport aircraft flying with the paratroopers somewhere over Europe. I am stationed in Southern Italy on the Foggia plain as a nose gunner on a B-24 heavy bomber of the 451st Bombardment Group.

At this juncture of my tour of duty, I have been credited with 10 missions and 17 sorties, received my first Air Medal and Purple Heart. The month of November was my favorite—I SURVIVED!

During this morning's briefing, we are told this winter has been the worst winter recorded in 60 years! Freezing temperatures, cold, harsh rains with ice and sleet, snow, and—worst of all—mud up to our ankles that makes walking at times almost impossible. I don't feel so sorry for myself when I think of the G.I.'s ("dogfaces") on the front lines in their foxholes, cold and wet, with mud up to their ears.

"The good news is," my commander's voice snaps me back to attention. "We will not be flying any missions on this day and on Christmas day because bad weather conditions over our target areas have hampered the success of our missions."

This news is worth a celebration—and celebrate we do! On Christmas Eve my crewmates and I go to the squadron enlisted men's club to join the Christmas festivities. I am not a drinker of alcoholic beverages, but my crewmates entice me to have a couple of Italian cherry brandies. The drinks are sweet and mellow, easy going down, and before the festivities end, I have more than a couple. We enjoy the party and at approximately 2400 hours, we leave the club, trudge to our tents, and hit the warmth of our "sacks." The cherry brandy takes its toll. Who undressed me? I have no idea. All goes suddenly quiet, and we are all a sound asleep. I snooze comfortably, secure in the knowledge that a well-deserved rest will follow.

Was I wrong!! At approximately 0300, the company clerk comes bursting into our tent and calls out our names. Each of us responds, knowing that we will fly a mission on Christmas day! "What happened to our day off from combat?" I ask myself. Later, during the day's briefing, we are told that the weather is clear over the target area. We are briefed to bomb the marshalling yards of Brux, Czechoslovakia,(one of the toughest target for the 15th AAF) located close to the border of Germany and north of Prague.

Four hours of high altitude flying followed—on oxygen and enduring extremely cold temperatures (-48 degrees C. with a wind chill factor of -134 degrees) Finally, we arrive at Brux. The target is completely obscured by cloud cover. The group leader decides to bomb an alternate target—the Wels, Austria marshalling yards. After another hour or so, we arrive over the target area. The weather is C.A.V.U. (ceiling and visibility unlimited). We hit the marshalling yards with 92% accuracy, knocking it out. (It is Our Christmas present to Hitler and his gang!) Flak is scattered and moderate. Our escort fighters (P-38's) are with us all the time. A Christmas present given to us from the 15th Air Force, I assume.

As the events of Christmas Day 1944 unfold, I must say it's not so bad after all. We all arrive back at our base safely, and I earn my 11th mission and 19th sortie.

If my luck holds up, I should finish my tour of duty by April.
MERRY CHRISTMAS TO ALL!!

Note:

On the following two days, I continued to fly more missions.

Date	City	Country	Target	Pilot	Time
Dec. 26, 1944	Oswiecim	Poland	Synthetic Rubber Plant	H.S. Patterson	8.5 hrs.
Dec. 27, 1944 (My second milk run—Yippee!!)	Venzona	Italy	Viaduct	H.S. Patterson	5.5 hrs.

HAPPY NEW YEAR!!!

SORTIE

FIFTEENTH AIR FORCE • PRINTED IN ITALY ; FREE DISTRIBUTION

VOL. I No. 1 - SUNDAY, 24 DECEMBER 1944

15TH HITS NAZI OIL

MERRY CHRISTMAS

WITH A WREATH TO SGT. SANSONE
CHIEF, WOLF

SORTIE

FIFTEENTH AIR FORCE

VOL. I No. 1 · SUNDAY, 24 DECEMBER 1944 · · · PRINTED IN ITALY ; FREE DISTRIBUTION

15TH HITS NAZI OIL

Downs 55 Planes During Busy Week

A week of bombing by instrument was climaxed Friday with publication of photo interpretation of the five major targets attacked, all of them synthetic oil plants.

The score as shown by the reconnaissance was two victories—at Bretthammer, a probable—at Oswiecim, a possible—at Brux, and a miss at Oderial.

Crewmen had a very busy day on Sunday, when 150 enemy aircraft attacked on the way to Silesia.

A Liberator group suffered heavily. The Luftwaffe lost a total of 55 to the gunners and fighter pilots. Flak continued to be heavy at the big targets.

The Sunday battle was the biggest for the air force since August 22 when 150 fighters attacked formations also attacking Silesian targets. The 15th shot down 47 that day.

The Fighter Command established two records on Sunday. It put more Mustangs and Lightnings over Germany than it ever has before, and it the boundaries of pre—war Germany, shoving up locomotives and other items (including a trolley car).

with the mission to knock on Saturday the 16th and continued for five days. It came at a timely time as the German tanks and aircraft staged a break through on the Western Front.

The Wehrmacht now has only two major sources of oil fuel left to it, the synthetic oil plants inside Germany and a natural oil basin in western Hungary. Once it had a third, the Rumanian oil fields, neutralized by the 15th in the Battle of Ploesti.

Within range of the heavy bombers from Italy are the natural oil refineries of Austria and Hungary. These have nil

GENERAL TWINING WELCOMES SORTIE

Major General Nathan F. Twining, Commanding General of the Fifteenth Air Force, has sent to the staff of *Sortie* a message for the personnel of the 15th AAF and associated units.

The text of the message follows:

«I welcome *Sortie* to the family of the 15th Air Force.

«This is your paper. It will contain news of all units, as well as personal features and general news. Its success will depend upon the cooperation given it by all echelons of command.

«To *Sortie's* staff, my best wishes ».

Maj. Gen. Nathan F. Twining

LATE WORLD BULLETINS

(Released by PWB through United Nations News Service).

SHAEF, PARIS, December 23 (Reuters). — Saturday's communique from General Eisenhower's headquarters states:

"Allied forces in the Maas-han sector continued local engagements with no substantial change in the position. In the vicinity of Haten the troops had gained a small amount of

Congressmen Inspect 15th AAF Units

15th AAF.—This headquarters was host to members of the House Military Affairs committee, as they made the final swing on a tour of European battle fronts.

Major General Nathan F. Twining, 15th AAF commander, welcomed the party on its arrival in Southern Italy after a visit to the Fifth Army front.

24 at ves were shown the facilities and intricate workings that enable this command to maintain a systematic bombing of Germany.

The Committee paid tribute to the excellence of the command and the morale of the Air Corps. They expressed appreciation of the adverse weather conditions and praised the over-all effectiveness of the 15th AAF.

At the conclusion of their visit here, Representative John M. Costello, of California, who was acting chairman stated that the committee planned to visit

Achi. Mary

Nicholas

The T. Kozakis'

1941 — 1946

JOHN   DEC. 1941 - 1945
NICHOLAS MAR. 1942 - 1946
ACHILLES JAN. 1944 - 1946
MILTON JUL. 1944 - 1946

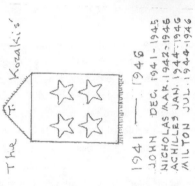

Milton

Pa. Thomas

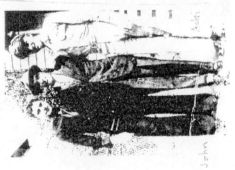

John

'Twas the night before Christmas, he lived all alone, in a one bedroom house made of plaster and stone. Image here I had come down the chimney with presents to give, and to see just who in this home did live. I looked all about, a strange sight I did see, no tinsel. no presents, not even a tree. No stocking by mantle, just boots 6lled with sand. on the wall hung pictures of far distant lands. With medals and badges; awards of all kinds, a sober thought came through my mind. For this house was different. it was dark and dreary. I found the home of a soldier, once I could see clearly. The soldier lay sleeping, silent, alone. curled up on the floor in this one bedroom home. The face was so gentle, the room in such disorder. not how I pictured a United States Soldier. Was this the hero of whom I'd just read? Curled up on a poncho, the floor for a bed? I realized the families that I saw this night. owed lives to these soldiers who were willing to fight. Soon round the world the children would play. and grownups would celebrate a bright Christmas day. They all enjoyed freedom each month of the year. because of the soldiers like the one lying here. I couldn't help wonder how many lay alone. on a cold Christmas Eve in a land far from home. The very thought brought a tear to my eye. I dropped my knees and started to cry. The soldier awakened and I heard a rough voice, "Santa don't cry, this life is my choice; I fight for freedom, I don't ask for more, my life is my God, my Country, my Corps." The soldier rolled over and drifted to sleep, I couldn't control it, I continued to weep. I kept watch for hours, so silent and still and we both shivered from the cold night's chill. I didn't want to *leave* on that cold night. this guardian of honor so willing to fight. Then the soldier rolled over, with a voice soft and pure, whispered, "Carry on Santa, it's Christmas day, all is secure. One look at my watch and I knew he was right. "Merry Christmas my friend, and to all a good night.

Anonymous

In case we find ourselves starting to believe all the anti-American Sentiment and negativity, we should remember England's Prime Minister Tony Blair's words during a recent interview. When asked by One of his Parliament members why he believes so much in America, he Said:

> "A simple way to take measure of a country is to look at how many Want in . . . And how many want out." Only two defining forces have Ever offered to die for you:
>
> 1. Jesus Christ
> 2. The American G. I.
>
> One died for your soul, the other for your freedom."

YOU MIGHT WANT TO PASS THIS On, AS MANY SEEM TO FORGET BOTH OF THEM.

THE REC ROOM

Winter in southern Italy can sometimes be extremely harsh. It is cloudy, wet, and cold; the penetrating winds bite without mercy. Such was the day I visited the Rec Room.

The Recreation Room is a musty, cold, damp and empty place, void of any people. One lonely bulb hangs helplessly from a wound cord attached to a brass socket as if to say, "turn me on and warm my soul."

A table, a bench and several chairs complete the interior furnishings. No heating was available. Perhaps this is the reason there's no one present. A single window located on the far end wall, most likely placed there for ventilation, collects dust along its edges for the next "spring cleaning."

A quick survey of the room reveals, in the far corner, a table with a dusty & drab record player and scattered around it are perhaps an even dozen recordings. It's evident by the growth of dust and cobwebs that these have sat motionless for sometime. The webs, of course, make a good home for the lonely spider that light on the chair nearby.

Having no source of music, no radio or recordings of my own, I am delighted by the find that would make up for the last two months, void of any euphony. It doesn't matter what the recordings were. All that mattered is that it's *music*. But upon closer inspection and to my delighted surprise, the records contain several classical tunes and a variety of current pop songs and instrumentals, songs like *Let Me Love You Tonight, I'll Be Seeing You, Stardust, One O'Clock Jump, Praise the Lord and Pass the Ammunition*, and several other tunes of the early forties. Man, what luck! Someone must be watching over me. As my Aunt Bessie said, "God will always be with you." God bless Aunt Bessie!!

As it turned out, most of my leisure hours were well spent in this cold, lonely and most uncomfortable room. But I realized it was not the first impression of the environment that gave me these precious moments of relaxation. It was the warmth and joy I felt listening to this bonanza of newly found, wonderful music.

The classics like *The Warsaw Concerto* and *The 1812 Overture* would always uplift my spirits when I was feeling low. Some of the recordings were soft, mellow and romantic like *Stardust*. Hoagie Carmichael wrote the music during the late thirties, and it was played as an instrumental for the first few years. Then Mr. Parish took the melody and wrote the lyrics with the introduction. I'm sure, Mr. Parish was in love at that writing. The introduction is the clue. Today, *Stardust* is still a classic. A favorite jitterbug tune like the *One O'clock Jump* that I danced to through my last year of high school, and of course, *I'll Be Seeing You*, were big hits with everyone. At times, this would bring a tear rolling down my cheek, stirring my loneliness and love for my family back home.

The recordings I found imbued me with a sense of solitude and relaxation. My imagination created an atmosphere of "sunny Italy" and with that a warm, restful, happy-to-be-alive feeling and the satisfaction of a few deserving golden moments of peacefulness. For now, the war will have to wait, at least for a while.

Note: Later I had learned that mostly all serviceable equipment and furnishings were requisitioned and installed in the new Enlisted Men's Club that opened in Dec 1944.

LONELINESS

(When "mail call" does not call you)

"I wish I knew some one like you to love me."

"Will I ever find a girl in my arms—a girl that is my ideal?"

"In my arms, in my arms, will I ever get a girl in my arms?"

"Let me love you tonight while the moon up above shines a heavenly light."

The aforementioned lines or verses are from the romantic ballads written and recorded during the war years of 1942 through 1945. These songs played in juke boxes and on the radio filled many of my empty, lonely hours. I was an inexperienced, romantic young soldier of 20 years who had not tasted the fruits of romance and love making. I would even venture to say, I was in that 60 to 70 percent of young men serving their country. We were mostly recent high school graduates or farm boys who volunteered or were drafted into military service. As for me, there was no time for girls, no time for romantic games, and no time to venture into the ritual "hunt."

Let's face it: I was a shy young guy with lots of dreams but no action. A casual conversation or a dance or two with a member of the opposite sex was a big deal. I'm sure every G.I. wanted a girl to write home to and most importantly to receive a letter from in return.

To say it bluntly, I needed a girl to talk to and one to love.

During my combat days, the immutable "mail call" was the main event, the highlight of the day! (Even better than chow or sack time). Especially if you were fortunate enough to get a letter from a girlfriend or your family back home. Many days, I would return to my tent without an ounce of mail, feeling sorry for myself. Yes, we would joke about "mail call" in various ways, but down deep inside of me it was no laughing matter (like the song—"laughing on the outside and crying on the inside . . ."). The loneliness lingered as the pain deepened within me. I would strain to smile and force a soft chuckle upon my crewmates trying to camouflage my true feelings. It was not easy!

Assurance is essential for a lonely G.I. When you are assured by someone or something, combat and loneliness are a little more tolerable.

Eventually, more often than not, I would leave the crew and the warm comfort of my tent and stroll to the forlorn, cold and retired "Rec" room which at one time was a bustling, fashionable squadron hang-out. In this private harbor I would sit and listen to the few dispersed recordings (spoils of war) left behind when the new enlisted men's club was opened. This precious euphony would mend the pain of my loneliness, again and again.

FACING DEATH AND I DIDN'T KNOW IT

Facing death and I didn't know it!

It never happened to me before. How could I recognize it?

Shortly after our return from the day's mission, Page Rodriguez, our tail gunner, and I visited Lauren Balzer, our ball turret gunner and patient at Foggia General Hospital. Lauren was being treated for a collapsed lung received during the mission from a dislodged, malfunctioned oxygen hose and consequently a loss of precious oxygen. He seemed to be O.K. except for a few occasional grunts and the discomfort he felt resulting from the medical equipment he was connected to.

As I gaze around the ward and next to Lauren's bed, I notice a patient whom I've never met before, stretched over a gurney with two nurses and a medic orderly furiously working over him. Suddenly, he rises off his back, startling the nurses and medic as his actions take them by surprise.

Staring straight into my eyes and simultaneously pointing his finger at me, with a raspy yet determined voice, he asks, "Who is he?" Momentarily, the nurses calm the patient. I can hear their whispers explaining to him that I am "a soldier, like you, just visiting a buddy".

His white complexion matching his gray, piercing, yet hollow eyes, gaze at me, and, for an instant, it seems that I can see completely through them. I'm chilled by his look!!

Moments later I return to Lauren's bedside and continue our visit assuring him that all is well with him and the crew.

The next morning we didn't fly (stand down) giving me an opportunity to visit Lauren again. I found him sitting up in bed within an oxygen tent. His mood was pleasant and we joked about the previous mission. My curiosity about the other patient came into our conversation and I asked Lauren about his neighbor. He was not aware of the very ill patient next to this bed.

I just could not delete this patient from my thoughts or feelings. I asked the nurse, who was making a new bed next to Lauren's about the patient I encountered the previous evening. She sorrowfully responded "he passed away a few minutes after you left". For a moment I felt traumatized by his death, yet I never knew where, how, or what brought about his demise.

I sat next to Lauren without saying a word for a couple of minutes. Then looking into Lauren's eyes, I just knew he would recover. Thanks to the great care and attention he was receiving from the doctors and dedicated nurses. My visit was short and a numb feeling overcame me as I headed out for the gate to hitch a ride back to our airbase.

HOMEWARD BOUND

Nearing the identifiable landmarks of the Italian boot spread out below, a sense of comfort and safety from marauding fighters and flak builds within me as I suck up a deep breath of oxygen within my mask and sigh with a "thank you, Lord." Our box formation was lucky on this mission. No major flak damage could be observed as I scanned the aircraft wingtips, left and right. The Squadron leader begins his descent and we follow like a flock of geese heading south for the winter.

I unbuckle and slip off my oxygen mask, reset my heating suit control to a more comfortable temperature, and turn on the radio to the Foggia-Allied Armed Forces Radio Station,(Pat would always turn on the radio for our pleasure) just in time to hear the announcer say, as always, "This is Allied Armed Forces Radio overlooking downtown Foggia." In return, I would always retort with a loud chuckle, *". . . . most of downtown Foggia"*. This area was flattened by the enemy and the Allies that came here before my arrival.

Minutes later we're flying over our base and the crew is preparing for landing. Our box executes an echelon maneuver: each aircraft is spread out wingtip-to-wingtip. The leader then peels off with a sharp bank to the left and the remaining aircraft follow. Thus each craft is in its proper position for landing within the specified time and without flying into the prop wash of the aircraft in front. Soon we are landing and a grateful happy-to-be-alive feeling overcomes me while savoring the smell of whorls of smoke from burnt rubber being sucked into the forward bomb bay where I'm standing as the tires touch down on the steel mat runway. The bomb bay doors have been cracked open prior to landing and I'm ready to start the generator when the aircraft comes to a halt at the end of the runway. We then begin to taxi to our designated revetment.

The ground crews, mechanics, armorers, tin tapers and radio men are anxiously waiting to inspect and service "their" aircraft. Ground crews and air crews alike, "take possession" of the aircraft and all call it their own. In my book, we fly it, they maintain it and keep it flying, and Uncle Sam (the taxpayer) owns it, so we can all say with pride, it's "our" airplane.

MY HEROES OF THE 451ST

Southern Italy along the Adriatic coast during the winter of 1944-45 was a challenge to our well being and survival. The frequent change in weather patterns was quick, cold and wet and the merciless prevailing winds off the Adriatic Sea gave us no quarter. There were times however, when the sun, peaking through the broken gray clouds would bless our soul with much needed warmth and provide us with a vitamin D boost to nourish our deprived body. Should we for any reason, venture into the shade on an infrequent sunny day, the sun's warm rays would suddenly disappear and the temperature would turn frigid.

To compound the miserable experience of a winter's cold, wet and foggy day or night, a black quagmire engulfed the area and would undoubtedly stick to our pants and boots as we tried to move about. No, this was not the time to venture out of the comfort of our tent. It was best to stay in our sack!

Being a member of an aircrew, I realized that not flying on days like this, had its advantages. I would opt to stay in my warm and dry tent, writing letters to my folks and other loved ones back home while enjoying the comfort of my sack or just make up rumors to exchange with other rumormongers I met in the mess hall or in the latrine.

My thoughts & concerns, however, were for the extraordinary breed of men known as the "ground crews" who did their work endlessly or so it seemed, day in, day out, night in, night out, rain or shine! The ground crews, responsible for maintaining the aircraft—be it replacing an engine; filling the tanks with petrol, oil, oxygen or hydraulic fluid; loading bombs and ammunition; or patching the skin of the airplane that returned from a mission looking like a sieve on wings with wheels—in my opinion, did not receive the attention, or recognition they so justly deserved. The dedicated ground crews were my **Heroes**, for without them, we (air crews) would never get off the ground!

Several times while on guard duty (after the British troops left the area, air crews not flying would be assigned to guard duty), I would watch the ground crews working their assigned jobs in the most arduous conditions. There were no hangers or sheds to protect them from the severe weather. If they were fortunate, a canvas cover fluttering in the wind was all the protection they had. There were no concrete revetments or tarmacs, just a steel mat covering an 8 inch thick base of crushed sandstone (Kalichi) that provided the foundation over an existing wheat field. Pools of rain water dotted the revetment and should any of us slip and fall, it was a sure bet we arose cussing and wet. To add salt to the wound, our buddies had the laugh of the moment.

Of the many ground crew personnel, two stand out in my mind. I remember very well one member of the ground crew for the aircraft "Patches." He was Albert R. Baril, a graduate of Lynn Classified High School, Class of '39. I was also a graduate of the same school in the Class of '43. In high school, we affectionately called him "Boogie." He was a burly, heavy weight champion wrestler and long distance (cross country) runner. Boogie was a very conscientious ground mechanic and an all-around good guy. Whenever we, our crew, were flying a mission, Boogie would be sweeping out our tent and making up our bedrolls and always "sweating out" our return.

Joe Cancila was another member of the ground crew personnel, a ground armorer, always loading the aircraft with bombs, sometimes changing bombs from one type to another (500 to 1000 lbs and vice versa) during the same winter night. His hands were always bruised or chaffed and he would assist the flying crews without being asked and without hesitation.

Usually the flying crews were located at one area of the squadron and the ground crews at another area. If our (air crews') tents were spread out in the squadron area, the squadron clerk would have a difficult and time consuming procedure when alerting the air crews for their mission assignments. The ground crews were located close to their jobs and their vehicles. The mess hall and operations buildings were centrally located within the squadron area.

Many times arriving at our assigned revetment, I would see the aircraft standing ready and able for the day's mission, yet seemingly, thick shrouds of gray mist hugged the aircraft that would give way to trickling tears running down its sides and forming puddles on the steel mat below. We knew then it was a wet night for the ground crews.

"NOT ALL THE HEROES WERE PILOTS"

Top Row: Left: Albert R. "Boogie" Baril, Class of '39
Ground Mechanic for Aircraft "Patches" Tin Tappers Delight (726th)
Top Row: Center: Emie Thyberg, Class of '39
Waist Gunner, Shot down on his 3rd mission, POW (726th)
Top Row: Right: A. Kozakis, Class of '43
Nose Gunner, Completed Tour of Duty
35 Missions/54 Sorties (726th), LIFE MEMBER of the
"Lucky Bastard Club".
Bottom Row: Left: Charles Chronopolis, Class of '39
Ground Gunnery Headquarters & Link Trainer Instructor (451st)
Bottom Row: Right: Sisko Webster, Mass.
Gunner. Same crew as Emie. Same result.
Shot down on 3rd mission, POW (726th)

VIENNA: CITY NOT OF MY DREAMS

On February 7, 1945: My Mission No. 17, (29th Sortie) :Our Group was made up of two flights. Red to Vienna, Austria Petrochemical Plants and Blue to the Bratislava, Czhcoslovakia Docks located along the Danube River. The targets are 180 miles from each other. We are in the Red Flight.

Four plus hours have passed since take off without incident. No flak, no fighters, just the comforting and assuring murmur of four precious engines. The weather to the target is C.A.V.U.(Ceiling And Visibility Unlimited) Our primary strike point for today: the oil refineries just north-east from the city center of Vienna. Always, rough, and dreadful to all who dare to enter the flak ring, with its grey ghostly flak towers and blistering with 800 guns in the Vienna Area. Consisting of, 88, 105 and 128 mm anti-aircraft batteries.*This is my third mission to Vienna and like every Vienna mission this is no milk run!!

Our formation is made up of several groups of the 15th Air Force. This day, our squadron, the 726th of the 451st Bomb Group is leading the formation. 1st Lt. Harold S. Patterson's crew (my crew), with some of the "top brass," are in the lead ship. I'm flying with another crew as I was replaced by a navigator. The navigator took my position in the nose turret of my plane, thus the origin of the term "nose gator." I, in turn, fly nose gunner with Lt. Donald F. O'Connell's crew in the "Dog," box position, a "seat" just behind and slightly below the lead ship "Able." It is a well established fact that flying the box can have terrible consequences. Anti-aircraft batteries tracking the lead bird almost invariably hit the box position first. "Oh, what would I give to be flying with my crew this day?"

I sigh, taking in a deep breath of oxygen.

The I.P. (Initial Point of the Bomb Run) is minutes away. The group tightens its formation. Wing tip to wing tip, tail to nose, the aircraft "suck it up" for a good bombing pattern and to discourage any enemy fighters that may be lurking about.

---

* During the month of November, 1944, we were briefed that flak guns around the Vienna area were 680 in number. The successful Russian campaign during the months of December through February, 1945, captured the surrounding battlefronts; therefore, more guns were transferred to protect the Vienna area targets from Allied and the 15th Air Force Bomb Groups.

Fighters usually don't mess with a tight formation because of its tremendous concentration fire power from 50 caliber machine guns. They prefer a scattered formation for easy penetration.

We turn on the I. P. radio, silence follows except for the bombardier telling the pilot he has taken control of the aircraft. Approximately four minutes pass, nothing but silence except for the engines and slipstream rushing past. No flak! Are we going to pass the flak batteries & towers below without incident? "Oh God, I hope so."

The words "Bombs Away!" shatter the silence as our ship lifts slightly and the bombs free fall to the intended target. Simultaneously, sudden fury breaks the long wait. Lt. Naylor (Pilot) in the deputy lead ship receives a direct hit! It rises above me, slightly to my right and I can see a hole beneath the flight deck large enough to accommodate a jeep. The aircraft continues to rise for a second or two, then turns on its back and down it goes. Down, down, damn it down! Milliseconds pass, then we're hit with the same round of bursts. The No. 2 engine is on fire, then extinguished and feathered. Our ship loses another engine, the left wing vibrates wildly, the aircraft turns left, then pitches down. The steepness of the turn increases as we fall, the centrifugal force bears against my body. Down we go with flak tracking our crippled ship. At the 2 o'clock position, 1-2-3 black bursts crackle and are blushed with a smell of deadly spent powder. Burst after burst, ever closer. Will the next burst be our last? "Dear Lord," I ask, "Why don't they track the Group and leave us alone?"

We continue to fall, heading for the center of Vienna as the blue copper dome of St. Karlskirche (St. Charles Church) rapidly expands and rises to meet us.

I turn my turret 30° starboard and witness the No.3 engine being feathered. I call for the Pilot, no sound greets me, our radio is shot, no intercom, nothing but the wind and flak trying ever so hard to reach its target—**us!!** Within seconds No.4 engine is trailing smoke leaving us with **one** engine over Vienna!

Falling, falling, still falling and then suddenly at approximately 17,000 feet, the aircraft levels off with the No.4 engine turning without full power and with a runaway supercharger. Pilot, Lt. O'Connell, and the Co-Pilot, Lt. Hovestreydt, get one engine in operation, leaving us with two. I turn my turret to find the Navigator and Bombardier through the glass slots of my outer turret doors. **No sign of them!!** Panic fills my turret. Confused and terrified, I scan the area looking down to the escape crawl space leading to the open bomb bays, nose well and flight deck. There I see somebody's rear end and the two soles of his boots saying "goodbye" as he frantically thrashes towards the open bomb bays. My heart sinks, "God Almighty, the bastards left me locked in my turret," I shout. "This would have never happened flying with **my crew**." Hurriedly, I turn my turret forward 0° Azimuth, and begin to open the turret doors without difficulty. Suddenly and to my amazement and horror, the outer doors are locked. I'm trapped, no way out and no parachute!! Frantically, I beat at the door with my back—nothing gives. I was so fearful of this moment and yet, had always believed it would never happen to me! The blue copper dome below propels closer and closer. We continue to lose cherished altitude.

Controlling my fears, I lower my guns thus raising my seat and turning my turret completely to my left with my head bearing on the turret's Plexiglas dome. I catch the wide-eyed Pilot, Lt. O'Connell. He sees the fear in my eyes and waves me the "high sign," calming my fears and assuring me that "all is well—don't worry, we've got the aircraft under control."

"Thank the Lord," I pray, as I see Aunt Bessie's face before me making a sign of the cross and blessing me saying, "A-chillea, God will always protect you." He truly has been with me!

We struggle for home with a runaway turbo, no radio communications, shot hydraulic systems, no flaps, no brakes and bomb bay doors that are locked in the open position.

Exhausted and with a deep sigh of relief, I rotate my turret once again—raise my guns and continue through observation to scrutinize the wings and engines, concluding that we have only **two** engines to carry us home!

Little did I know during those horrible agonizing seconds, that the Navigator, Lt. Austin, went to the flight deck to navigate from that position because our radio and intercommunications were disabled. Lt. Hayes, the Bombardier, left his position to check the damage inflicted on the aircraft. However, these questions return to my mind, "Why didn't they unlock my outer doors and why didn't they tell me 'why' they were leaving their respective positions?"

Minutes have passed, but it seems like hours. We are beyond the range of Vienna's deadly flak towers and anti-aircraft batteries as we lumber our way to our air base about 480 miles south. The Alps are ahead of us and we continue to lose precious altitude. Will we clear the peaks of the snow-capped Austrian Alps? "Dear Lord, please stay with us today," I whisper to myself. My thoughts momentarily flash back to watching our deputy lead bomber receive a direct hit. I didn't want to think of what horrors were unfolding in the helpless aircraft with its doomed crew.

The sweat crystallizes down my back (I'm freezing but can't feel it); the worries resume. Separated from the formation, my eyes scour the skies gazing for enemy aircraft. Our crippled plane is like nectar to the bee, easy prey for enemy fighters, alone, cold, wounded and slowly straggling home. My prime concern is the safety of our aircraft and its crew, yet, in my nose position, isolated as I am, locked in my turret with no radio contact with the crew, I feel abandoned and hopeless, even though, my extensive training and experience taught me otherwise!

I continue with my watchful duties—scanning the skies for fighters—friend or foe. The former would be most welcome. Pressing the intercom button again and again, I try to contact the flight deck. Nothing. No sound but the background noise of the air stream passing over and around my turret and the murmur of our two precious engines. If I should discover enemy fighters, how would I alert the crew? This horrible scenario crosses my mind.

The Austrian Alps loom larger, approximately 5 miles ahead of us as I clearly see the snow-capped peaks and the exposed ragged mountain sides, a reminder of our precarious condition. Our descent slowly but surely diminishes considerably as the peaks and ridges are passing below with several hundred yards to spare. "How much longer will our two precious engines continue to fly us home?" I ask myself.

Unknown to me, the crew members in the waist position had jettisoned all guns, ammunition, flak suits, anything that had weight to lighten the aircraft.

I continued to scan the clear blue sky above me and the horizon below. Nothing but C.A.V.U. A comforting feeling overcomes my fears. Turning the turret to a 1 o'clock position and lowering my guns, I discover two black spots at 2 o'clock high. Subconsciously I press the intercom button to alert the crew. Nothing—I'm reminded again—the radio is shot out! Within seconds the black images become silhouetted fighters. "Friend or foe?" flashes through my mind, the adrenaline builds within me, my heart is beating like a kettle drum. Two or three seconds pass—the fighters do not maneuver into a pursuit curve nor do they maneuver for a head-on attack. Instead, they are sliding into my position and slightly ahead of me to my right side. At this instant I recognize the red tails, the blue and white star and bar, the air scoop below and their red noses. At approximately 150 yards distance and within a second of time I confirm the fighters are **ours**!! Two P-51 escort fighters attached to the 332 Fighter Group—The Tuskegee Airmen.[*] Our Red Tail Angels!!

I turn my turret slightly to my left, away from the fighters, simultaneously lowering my twin 50 caliber machine guns. "Don't screw-up, Kozakis," I murmur to myself. "Don't scare our friends away." (Some trigger happy gunners would shoot anything within sight and you would not see an escort fighter for a week!) One fighter aircraft, the wing man, is flying above us at about 1,500 yards in a crisscross pattern, while the lead escort fighter continues to slide toward our right wing. At this vantage point I see the pilot's head in his bubble canopy. He wiggles his wings. I, in turn, wave at him; he responds with the "hi sign" and pulls away about 300 yards. "Joy, oh sweet joy!" Euphoria overcomes me. "Safe at last," I shout. The red painted tails, the red noses with painted yellow stripe on the top side of their wings will never leave my mind.[**] A sight I'll never forget!

No enemy aircraft were lurking about and the Tuskegee Angels were shepherding us to our base, giving me encouragement and protection; a most precious moment to savior.

We flew together, a crippled bomber and two Tuskegee escort P-51 fighter aircraft. We passed the Yugoslavian mountains, away from enemy fighter territory.

---

[*] The 332 Fighter Group of the 15th Air Force, affectionately know by the bomber crews and recognized as the "Tuskegee Angels" and "Red Tailed Angels." The Fighter Group comprising the 99th, 100th, 301st, 302nd Fighter Squadrons, never lost a bomber while providing escort missions during the entire air war.

[**] The yellow wing striping used to make P-51's more easily recognized in the Middle Eastern and Italian theater of operations.

The flight engineer, T. Sgt. Casmier J. Czachorowski, finally unlocks my turret doors and signals that I leave my position and assist him to repair flak damage. We're flying at approximately 14,000 feet. The bomb bay doors cannot be closed, the incoming air stream is about 39°F below zero. (The wind chill factor is minus 114 degrees) Hustling, without oxygen masks and parachutes, we begin trying to repair the hydraulic system. The lines are cut and the fluid within the storage tank spurts into my face and hands and eventually I'm drenched with hydraulic fluid from my head to the bottom of my back. My B-10 jacket is dripping with fluid. Momentarily Zack thought it was blood!

I was a potential Molotov cocktail and never realized it at that time.

Hastily we tie some of the control cables with bailing wire requisitioned from the bomb bays. This joint effort strengthened the cables somewhat. My hands and face are frostbitten and, to a degree, frozen numb. Momentarily, we become immobilized, short of oxygen and exhausted. We continue with our repairs until the bombardier motions us to return. We crawl to the flight deck just in time to see our friends leaving their positions and flying off to their base located north of Foggia. We're flying over the Adriatic Sea at about 5,000 feet and the Italian coast line is a few minutes away.

FISH OR CUT BAIT

The situation is very grave and no one available on the flight deck (Flt. Engineer, Bombardier, or Navigator) can manually lower the landing gear. Our hydraulic system was destroyed by enemy flak over the target. Time is running out! Making it back to the airfield we're making our approach and flying the downwind leg of our landing pattern. Lt. O'Connell has to make a decision within two to three fleeting short minutes:

DO WE JUMP OR DO WE CRASH LAND??

I hastily crawl up to the flight deck from the bomb bays and standing behind the pilot's seat, I observe the distance and change of height between the landing gear hand crank and space behind the pilot's seat. I surmise that I can plunge on the hand crank from this position, and by grasping the handle tightly, and with the weight and twisting momentum of my body, I could force the handle to turn. You don't think about it—"you just **do it**."

The crewmembers on the flight deck thought I was insane (or flak happy) to try this maneuver because I could not use my parachute and the bomb bay doors below were stuck in the open position. Should I miss the emergency landing gear hand crank, it was certain death. My imperturbable optimism was not to be dampened by failure, however great! It was a rash action that I didn't regret.

Without hesitation and with every ounce of adrenaline and fortitude my body possesses, neglecting for the moment my wounds and extreme pain, I plunge at the hand crank again and again until I can turn the manual hand crank freely. Suddenly, the wheels begin their descent. A free fall follows and simultaneously the hand crank spins like a propeller.

The landing gear comes down in the **locked** position!!

For a brief moment there is spontaneous chatter of relief on the flight deck. And, as a reward for my successful endeavor, Czachorowski (our flight engineer) allows me to fire the Very pistol, notifying the anxiously awaiting ground crews below that we were extremely damaged and with wounded crewmembers aboard.

Because of my extraordinary achievement and courageous actions beyond the call of duty, the pilot lands the airplane safely with no further damage to the crew or the plane. The aircraft comes to a stop at the end of the runway with only a few yards to spare.*

Instantly the crew members in the waist positions scramble out of the plane. The runway has a three degree slope causing the aircraft to roll backwards. (We have no brakes, no flaps and four dead engines.)

As the backward rolling motion of the aircraft begins to pick up momentum and speed, with no time to waste, I grab my parachute and jump to the steel mat runway below. I set my parachute at the landing wheel, choking the aircraft to a final stand still. Within seconds the pilot and remaining crew members remove themselves from the flak ridden aircraft.

Soon, after all crew members are out of the stricken aircraft, the adrenaline within me subsides and losing consciousness, I find myself on my back in the aid station. The Flight Surgeon and his medic are tending my wounds and telling me, "Kozakis, you earned a purple heart." Jokingly, I respond, "How about an aspirin instead Captain, I already have one" The room suddenly fills with laughter. The flight surgeon and medic finish bandaging my wounds.

Bandages cover my hands, lower arms, face and neck. I look like a mummy ready for entombment. I personally felt the men at the aid station gave me the V I P treatment. Of course, I was in no position to argue and I didn't. AS a matter of fact, I rather enjoyed all the attention and comfort bestowed upon me.

---

* A few days later Lt. O'Connell told me he was recommending me for the D.F.C. (Distinguished Flying Cross) for my superior actions during that mission. Unfortunately, the award never did reach me. Two months passed on and in that time I completed my tour of duty (35 missions/54 sorties) and sailed home. I often wondered what happened to that elusive D.F.C. Many years later, 50 to be exact, I learned that all of my military records were lost in the fire that consumed two floors of the National Personnel Records Center (Military Personnel Records) located in the St. Louis, Missouri. Could this be the reason?

"VIENNA-CITY NOT OF MY DREAMS"

Vienna/Brataslava February 7, 1945
Petrochemical Plant and Docks

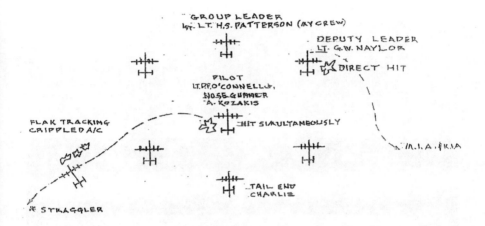

AT BOMBS AWAY!
(726th Bomb Squadron)

*   Straggling home with 2 Engines

726th Lost   1-aircraft and crew M.I.A. Lt. Gerald W. Naylor Pilot (P.O.W.)
725th Lost   5-aircraft and crews M.I.A. and K.I.A.
(Total this mission: 6 aircraft lost and crews K.I.A. and M.I.A. 25%)

*   Thanks to the Tuskegee "Red Tailed Angels," we made it home to fly again and again and again!

K.I.A. = Killed in Action
M.I.A. = Missing in Action

LANDING GEAR
EMERGENCY OPERATION

Main and Nose: The manual emergency system is used to lower and lock—IT WILL NOT RAISE—the main and nose landing gear in case of total failure of the main, auxiliary (electric) and emergency (hand) hydraulic systems. The operating crank is located on the forward center section spar on the centerline and can be reached from the forward end of

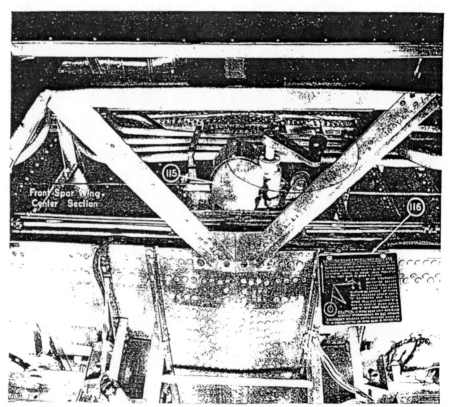

115. Landing Gear Hand Crank   116. Landing Gear Hand Crank Instructions

LEAVING VIENNA
WITH SMOKE & A PRAYER
(Feb. 7, 1945, 6 Aircraft Lost)

WELCOME BACK

The medic drives me to my tent, as I entered it was dark inside except for the glow of the stove, red hot and radiating heat within. All was quiet and my crew members were in their sacks asleep. I stumbled to my bunk about five feet from the right side of the tent entrance. My eyes became accustomed to the dark and the shadows of my crewmates became visible: Rodriguez and Balzer on my left, Carrington and O'Laughlin in the back and to the far side of the stove and Realley on my right in the far corner. Not a sound or word was heard except when my voice resonating within the tent.

"Couldn't you guys wait 24 hours before you clean out my bunk and possessions?!" I shouted. "Hell, I'm only a few hours late!" I continued as the tone of my voice became even louder.*

Rodriguez and Balzer awoke and responded, "We saw you go down Greek, with one engine feathered and another trailing smoke!" O'Laughlin, with his heavy Hibernian broghe, followed, "I saw no parachutes and you were still losing altitude—your plane fell out of formation!"

I felt the pain on my face as I tried to talk, then the talk became a giggle and then a laugh. Laughter began to reverberate within the tent as my crewmates were laughing with me. Simultaneously, they jumped out of their sacks, each returning my goodies (cigarettes, whiskey, candy and some extra blankets I had requisitioned) and replacing them in their original positions on my bunk.

Questions followed rapidly, I tried to answer but the medication was not relieving the pain as fast as I hoped it would.

"Fellas," I said, "get me undressed, please, and put me in the sack, we'll continue this tomorrow."

Within minutes I was out like a light.

Morning followed all too quickly and, man, was I hurting. More sleep was what I wanted and needed. Balzer came over with a canteen of water. Slowly and cautiously, I drank my fill. Carrington brought over some cookies he had received from home and O'Laughlin broke open a breakfast "K" ration for me. Realley and Rodriguez were covering my exposed feet with my blankets. I thought the boys were trying to kill me with kindness.

Pat, Tom, Burton and Bill (pilot, co-pilot, navigator and bombardier, respectively) visited that afternoon and, kidding, they all agreed that I would live and that I should be ready and on flying status within a few days. I'm sure they were just trying to lift my spirits and raise my moral.

---

* An agreement was made by all enlisted members of our crew that should any crewmember be missing in action, his belongings, such as cigarettes, candy, whiskey, etc., would be shared equally by the remaining crew members.

It is a well known fact that wounded air crew personnel were to be placed on flying status immediately upon any signs of recovery. I was treated no differently. I'm sure this strict procedure was for my benefit as well as for the war effort. If you're "sacked out" too long, you dwell on the possibility of not wanting to fly combat again. But this crosses your mind, injured or not.

A few days followed and the boys let me know through their actions that it was time for me to forget my wounds, get off my ass and be my eager self again. The honeymoon (short-lived as it was) was over. Soon, the adrenaline returned and Kozakis was ready to fly again. Our next mission was Moosebierbaum, Austria. An oil refinery located about 20-30 miles northwest of Vienna within range of the dreaded flak towers and guns and where this story began. I guess that's why they say war is hell.

St. Karlskirche, Vienna

October 1997: Looking out my hotel window I see the "Blue Dome".
I just had to see it, "close up" see photos above.
Refer to my story "Vienna City Not of my Dreams"

St. Karlskirche, Vienna

Augarten Flak Tower

Vienna Flak Towers
Recreation Facilities (Parks) are built
around the Towers. They are welded shut,
birds are the only trespassers.
Photos taken by A. Kozakis Oct. 1997.

Esterhazy L. Tower (South Side) Park

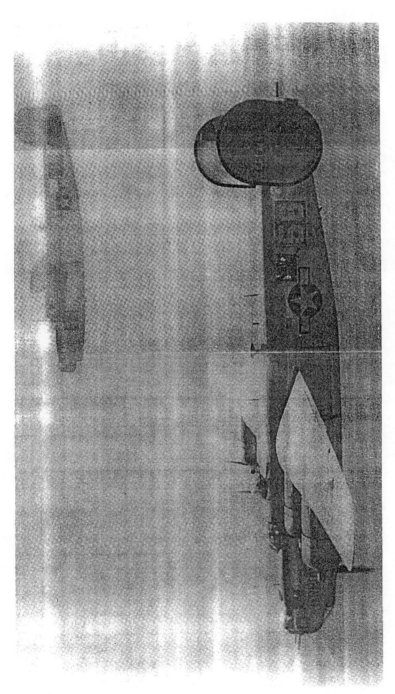

PILOT: O'CONNELL 1st LT.
NOSE GUNNER, KOZAKIS S. SGT.
"FLYING THE BOX POSITION"
TARGET: VIENNA, KORNEUBURG OIL
REFINERY, BRATISLAVA, PORT AREA

Rhoda, was B-24L 44-49866, from the 451st BG, 726th BS, with Battle Number 56. She arrived with the group on 15 December 1944. While on the 7 February 1945, mission, she sustained heavy flak damage, was repaired by the 60th Service Squadron, and returned to the group on 16 February. *Rhoda* made an emergency landing in Yugoslavia while on the 23 March 1945, mission to bomb the marshaling yards at Klagenfurt, Austria. Again she returned to the group on 26 March and returned to the 21 with the group. [via R. Karstensen]

MOMENTS TO CHERISH WHEN YOU'RE OLD AND GRAY

I have just completed a tough mission: the crew is intact, no one hurt.

I walk across the steel mat revetment, with my A-3 bag contain in my flying gear, to the awaiting truck or weapons carrier that will eventually take us (our crew) to post flight de-briefing.

Two Red Cross girls are awaiting our arrival with hot coffee and greasy donuts laid out on white paper in a container made from frag bomb boxes. Also waiting are the debriefing Intelligence officers (S-2) and the flight surgeon, serving a 2 ounce shot of 100 proof Rye Whiskey. Our ration for today's mission.

For an instant, you're walking on air!!

Then, moments later, reality sinks in and your gut is churning and grinding. Was it the donuts, the whiskey or the mission? It could have been the greasy donuts coated with sugar and washed down with the bitter coffee, grinds and all. You knew all too well that you'd experience a nauseated stomach in short order after consuming one or two to satisfy your ravaged hunger. Or it could have been the 2 ounce shot of Rye that exploded when it hit the bottom of your gut. After all, you landed with an empty stomach after flying for eight hours!! Even though the 100 proof Rye warms your insides, you're still cold on the outside. Sometimes your hands and face are blue and sometimes red, depending on whether your gloves and oxygen mask were heating and operating properly. Or just maybe, it was the mission itself.

The debriefing officer is asking questions about the mission and your thoughts revisit the moments you're trying to forget. You're cold, hungry and nervous and finally when you're excused you're ready for the sack or supper.

P.S. Many times I would skip supper and hit the sack for precious sleep only to be awakened at 0300 hours for the next day's mission. As they say, "War is hell."

VIGNETTES BY 'ACHI'

MOMENTS TO CHERISH WHEN YOU'RE OLD & GRAY

By Achilles Kozakis, 726th Bomb Squadron

I had just completed a tough mission, the crew is intact, no one hurt. Walking across the steel mat revetment, with my A-3 bag containing my flying gear, to the awaiting truck or weapons carrier that will eventually take us (our crew) to our post-flight debriefing.

Two Red Cross girls are awaiting our arrival with hot coffee and greasy donuts laid out on white paper atop a table made of frag-bomb boxes. Also waiting are the debriefing Intelligence Officers (S-2), and after that our Medics with a 2 ounce shot of 100 proof Rye Whiskey. Our ration for today's mission.

For an instant ... You're walking on air!

Then, moments later reality sinks in and your gut is churning and grinding from within. Was it the donuts, the whiskey or the mission? It could have been the greasy donuts coated with sugar and washed down with the bitter coffee, grinds and all. Or, it could have been the 2 ounces of Rye that exploded when it hit the bottom of your gut. After all, you landed with an empty stomach after flying for eight hours. Even though the 100 proof Rye warmed your insides, you're still cold on the outside. Sometimes your hands and face are red and sometimes blue, depending on whether your gloves and heated suit were heating properly. The donuts had their misgivings as well. You knew all to well that you'd experience nauseated stomach after consuming one or two to satisfy your ravaged hunger. Or, just maybe, it was the mission itself.

The debriefing officer is asking questions about the mission and your thoughts relive the moments your trying to forget. You're cold, hungry and nervous and when you're finally excused your ready for the "sack" or supper.

p.s. Many times I would skip supper and hit the "sack" for precious sleep, only to be awakened at 0300 hours for the next day's mission. They say war is hell!

ALL IN A DAY'S WORK (Written in early 1999)

On my way to Boston, flying at 29,000 feet in a DC-9, I was reminded of my earlier flights during WW-II. What struck me most was the space allocated for seating in the Economy Class Section.

The seat was no larger, or possibly even smaller, than that of an Emerson Nose Turret in a B-24H, Liberator bomber. I had, in my Emerson Turret, plenty of leg room to facilitate my cumbersome high altitude flying gear; boots, pants (2 pair), heated suit and gloves, B-10 jacket, goggles & oxygen mask, a Mae West, and last, but most importantly, my parachute harness.

Today's seating in the DC-9 would be most inadequate, for comfort, to say the least. The leg room for a 5'-11" person allows no space to move within the seat without disturbing your neighbor. The "dirty" looks one gets when shifting one's legs could be piercing. My flight took only 4 hour and 52 minutes. Thank God, I'm not on an eight hour mission to Ploesti.

Well, the war is over ... and I'll soon be reaching my destination. I'm pleased that I have nothing else to bitch about ... and they say war is hell!

Smile, it could be worse.

p.s. It's double-tough when the person in front of you lowers his back rest into your chest and the person behind is kicking your rear. Missions were never like this.

TYPICAL [AFTER MISSION] RED CROSS HOSPITALITY DONUT TABLE
(Locale/Squadron Unknown)

727th MEDICINAL WHISKY DISTRIBUTION TABLE
(Lt Peter Massare [w/cigarette] at right - others unknown)

Copy from the "Ad-Lib" (451st quarterly Publication)

NAPLES-MARCH 1945

Truly, March winds blow
Cold, crisp & biting
with moistened air from
the sea of Naples.

This day is gray
with dark clouds, drizzle
and no place to find cover.
A bad time to be out
in this cold dreary city.
Yet, there she stands
in a bombed-out doorway
finding little comfort.

Dark brown hair
tangle, twisted and wet
from gusts of drizzle.
Large dark hollow eyes
glancing and
following the passers by.

Her dress and shirt
wet and wrinkled
match her sandals
barely covering her cold feet.

Blue from the damp cold are
her lips, toes and fingers.

This G.I. watching can
No longer ignore.

Takes off his field jacket,
warm with his body's heat,
pulls off his sweater beneath
and dresses the young girl
with not an exchange of words.

For an instant I can
feel the glow of thanks and happiness upon her face.*

---

* In better times I'm sure those eyes were like sparkling olives.

The following is a copy of a letter I sent to my father during the war:

March 1, 1945

Hello Pa,

Just a few lines to let you know I am well and everything is O.K.!

You probably received my "Purple Heart" medal by now and I want to assure you that it will take more than a little flak to do me in. Just like "Ἀχιλλεὺς" I have one vulnerable spot and it's my heel. The German's don't know that!

We are having an extremely cold and wet winter. I am told it is the worst winter in 60 years! I believe them!!

We are well protected in our tent. Six of us, enlisted men in our crew, occupy a 16' x 16' tent with a stove made from a 55 gallon oil drum and a 75 millimeter shell casing. The shell casing is welded to the bottom of the steel drum and the shell casing has several 1/2" holes with pebbles at the bottom to catch the 100 octane gasoline (aviation fuel). As the gasoline is fed, drop by drop, onto the pebbles, it burns with a sound that lulls you to sleep. The steel drum gets cherry red and radiates heat throughout the tent—very warm and cozy.

Well Pa, I completed 21 missions and if all goes well, I should complete my tour of duty (35 missions) by the end of April, just in time to be home in the springtime, my favorite time of the year.

Your loving son,
Ἀχιλλεὺς

P.S.
The sketch shows how we built the stove

WHEN A GREEK MEETS A GREEK

Being members of replacement crew A-9 (H.S. Patterson's crew), we arrive at the 726th Bomb Squadron on October 20, 1944. Yes, the weather was wet, cold and the skies gray with heavy overcast. The Squadron's enlisted men, mostly were unhappy or I could say, downright mad about something. Most of the times when we arrived at a new station en route to the 726th, the G.I.s we met would be pulling pranks on us or making jokes. Lots of criss-cross chatter and light laughter. I whispered to Lauren, "Man, this place is like a morgue." "Yeah," he returned, "quiet and cold." Maybe the men were down because Thanksgiving and Christmas were not far off and they were here, far away from home, and the weather didn't help either.

We "settled in" for about a week or so and it dawned on me why morale of the Squadron was so low. Yes, it was the "chow!" Men would be grumbling and bitching as they waited in the chow line. "It can't get any worse, it has to get better," they would remind us.

Of course, our crew had several cases of "K" rations in our tent, the remains of our allotted rations issued to our crew for our use during the trip to our new "Permanent Station." These rations often would supplement the meals at the squadron mess hall and the local chow didn't bother us as much as it troubled the "permanent party" (Ground Crews) personnel.

Morale of the squadron was extremely low. They say "the army moves on its stomach," no words could be so true in describing the current condition of our squadron: They didn't move at all! I must admit, the chow was lousy—greasy, tasteless, salty; you name it, we had it!!!

Approximately three weeks passed and during that time we endured the agony of a miserable mess. I visited the bulletin board one morning and learned that a new mess crew would be assigned to the squadron per orders of Captain Henry E. Ford, Operations Officer. I was extremely pleased and the men surrounding me were overjoyed and enthusiastically joking about the announcement.

The new mess crew was met with apprehension by the men. It was not easy for the men to forget so quickly of their past experiences at the mess hall. A few trying days passed. Mostly all enlisted men in the squadron were gauges of how things were changing during this period. Morale and well-being of the men was uplifted and the frowning faces of the past gave way to smiles and laughing chatter. The chow lines grew longer and the men didn't mind the delay. The mess hall became an island of joy. Low morale of the enlisted men was no longer a problem.

Beef stew was great with its savory sauce (not grease) made thick and juicy for dunking your bread. Spam was camouflaged so that it was unknown to the recipient and the palate. My favorite, not served often enough, was the chicken soup with a lemon and egg (avgolemono) sauce. This was the Greek "Midas" touch they frequently introduced (if ingredients were available) to the Army menu. Whenever a shipment of fresh eggs (not powdered) arrived, probably once every three months, the cook would allow us to choose the method we wanted our eggs individually served: sunny side up, over easy, scrambled, boiled or any other method that time would permit. I often wondered, is this really the Army??

There is an old story that goes like this: When an Irishman meets an Irishman, they start a fight; and when a Greek meets a Greek, they open a restaurant.

The above describes the newly assigned cook and baker to the 726th Bomb Squadron. Both were first generation Americans of Greek ancestry (same as I). It wasn't long before I would frequent the mess hall and chat with my new buddies. They would, of course, always call me by my first name in Greek, "A-hillea" and I would respond with "Yias sas" (to your health) or "sto kallo" (to your well being) when I would leave.

It was the day after Christmas 1944, our crew (H. S. Patterson) returned late from our mission (Osweisim Poland-Sythetic Rubber Plant). The day was long and the mission extremely cold. After completing our post briefing, we were tired, cold, hungry and highly peeved when we found the mess hall doors closed. This meant no supper!

We returned to our tent and discussed our predicament. Do we stay and eat our "K" rations, which we accrued during our initial flight to the 726th Squadron? No! It was emphatically agreed by my five crew mates that Kozakis (the "Greek") would visit his buddies at the mess hall and requisition our supper.

I didn't want to impose on my recently found new "Greek" buddies (Tony—Mess Sgt. and Steve—Baker), but my stomach told me I was hungry and my crewmates would not have it otherwise.

With mess kit in hand, I trudge to the lonesome mess hall and find my buddies (cook and baker) making preparations for the next day's meals. As usual, they're happy to see me and after our warm, casual and friendly greetings, I explain my predicament and plead for our supper. Tony and Steve looked at each other, then give me a stern, foreboding stare.

"A-hillea, you know the rules—after the mess hall doors are closed, there are no meals."

Before I could rebuff and plead my case, they grabbed and hugged me like a long lost brother. "A-hillea, we can't let you or your crewmates go hungry," Tony said raising his voice. "Sit down and share a cup of coffee with us," replied Steve.

During their coffee break, Tony brought out a gallon can of turkey (I assumed saved from yesterday's Christmas dinner), a pound of butter and two loaves of bread.

"A-hillea, take this to your tent and with your crew mates enjoy your supper" Tony continued, "after flying all day, you shouldn't go to bed hungry. Steve inserted, "and leave your mess kit with me. I'm baking tonight."

Man, this was like being home with the family.

"I can't thank you enough for your kind generosity" I replied.

When I left with two arms full of goodies, they sent me off with "Sto Kallo" and "Kali Orexi." (To your well being and good appetite).

726th Mess Hall.

POLA

February 20 1945
19th Mission Pola, Italy German Naval Base Docks,
Shipping & Marshaling Yard

At approximately 0400 hours, the squadron clerk bursts into our tent, awakens us from dead sleep by calling our names. We acknowledge. This routine tells us we're flying today!

Completing our personal chores (dressing, latrine, washing & mess) we then wait for our pilot to arrive. Usually the gunners are briefed at the Squadron briefing room while the officers are briefed at Group Headquarters (GH). Today, however, it's different! Pat, my pilot, tells me I am to be briefed with the officers.

Upon my arrival to the Group Headquarters briefing room, I notice it was originally used by a previous owner of the farm as a wheat or wine storage building. It is approximately 35 feet wide by 80 feet long and has a vaulted ceiling about 16 feet high. A flight of stairs leads into a room below ground level. (I called it "the cellar." It would probably have made a good bomb shelter.)

The briefing room fills with air crew officers and their respective nose gunners. Lots of chatter fills the air and the overcrowded conditions seem to magnify the sound level. It is now about 0600 hours and our commanding officer, Col. Leroy Stefonowicz, along with the weather, intelligence and operations officers and their assistants arrive. "Attention!" the Captain's voice rings out. Silence follows as the Colonel and his entourage walk over to a make-shift stage with a back wall curtain obscuring our view from today's mission and routing. "At ease," the Colonel whispers, and the room sits in unison in anticipation of learning the day's targets.

As the curtain is gradually drawn, we can see the string partially showing the mission routing. Slowly, the target map comes into full view for everyone's curious mind to digest.

The target is the German Naval Base, Docks, Shipping & Marshaling yards located in Pola, Italy, just south of Trieste, a peninsula jutting into the Adriatic, southeast of Venice and into the Gulf of Venice on the east. We passed over this area many times on our previous flights, going and returning into southern Europe without incident. We always stayed a safe distance from their anti-aircraft batteries.

My first impulse was, at last a milk run! Was I wrong! I quickly learned the profound & vital importance of our target. This would not be a normal bomb run as an "attack unit," where every bombardier would salvo his bombs off of the lead ship. This mission was a "combat box run" (four waves of seven plane flights), a maximum effort. All squadrons would have one "box" of six to seven aircraft. Each box would make its individual bomb run and drop its bombs on an assigned target within the German Naval Base. Precise timing, tight box formations and target identification were the vital factors required for the success of this mission. Each bombardier with his respective nose gunner was being briefed as one unit (two sets of eyes are better than one). The briefings included use of photographs and maps of the target area. We were briefed on specific landmarks, buildings and harbor installations. This time, the briefing was more intense and time consuming. It was not the average type. Our target was a warehouse on the dockside and various ships were anchored adjacent to the warehouse. Other squadrons (724th, 725th, & 727th) had other chosen targets in the Naval Base, i.e. shipping, shops, marshalling yard and rolling stock. It was apparent that S-2 (Intelligence) spent a lot of time and effort compiling data and putting this mission together.

Col. Stefonowicz, our group commander, explains the importance of this particular mission. "We have an opportunity to strike the enemy where it would do the most damage to their supply of war material for their troops in Northern Italy. We're going to blast those bastards before their ships can leave the docks with cargo." Enthusiastic cheers and applause fills the room. Usually it is a quiet and calm atmosphere.

This mission was assigned to the 451st Bomb Group and it gave us an opportunity to "spread our wings!!"

The Operations officer and Group navigator brief us on the routing of our mission followed by the Weather officer and Intelligence officer. We will have clear weather, and the numbers of anti-aircraft guns over the target are not significant, but will be intense.

Bill Bodie (Lead Bombardier) and I review the data (photos of the target and map of the target area) and decide that I will alert Bill upon sighting the Naval Base from my Nose Gun Position. (Visibility is far greater from the Nose Turret than the Bombardier's position.) This will give Bill ample time to set his bombsight and prepare himself to hit and destroy the target.

Approximately four hours flying time have accrued and we are flying in a western direction, over the purple Yugoslavian mountains. Within a few minutes, I can see the Naval Base from my position. The target area is C.A.V.U. (Ceiling And Visibility Unlimited), a perfect atmosphere to bomb the assigned target. The Naval Base spreads along the Pola coastline and into the mainland for about a couple of miles. Ships of several types are anchored at dockside and in the bay. At approximately 1300 hours, I alert the crew and Bill that "I've sighted our target area." Moments later, we turn on the IP (Initial Point of the bomb run). I describe the target (warehouse at dockside) to Bill and he answers, "I have it." Radio silence follows. It's now up to Bill. He is in complete control of the aircraft. The success or failure of the mission depends on his actions in the short interval of the bombing run.

Flak becomes visible. At first, it is slight and off to our right side about two o'clock. Within a minute, hell breaks loose as the flak is intense and accurate. The aircraft bounces like a ball and the closer to the target we get, the heavier the flak grows.

"Bombs Away" breaks radio silence, a steep left rally gaining air speed, and leaving the target area behind. I automatically (force of habit) look right and left, checking the condition of our engines. All is O.K. except engine No. 3! It is blowing blue smoke.* I call Pat (our Pilot) on the interphone, and Tom (our Co Pilot) feathers No. 3 engine. We are losing power and cannot stay with the group. Burt Schilling (our Navigator) gives Pat a heading for home on three good engines.

I can see the havoc we spread along the dock side, the shop buildings and marshalling yard. The Naval Base is burning and smoke bellows into the sky below us as we head for our airfield.

Later we learned that Bill Bodie (Bombardier) made a "bulls-eye" on our specified target. We were told by Group that 47 tons of bombs obliterated the Naval Base and put it out of action for the duration of the war, and our box (Flight "B") had 100% hits, the best in the Group. Thereafter, Bill was known as "Dead Eye Bodie."

---

*   Upon returning to Base, the ground crew made their inspection of the engine and found flak had severed the oil line to No. 3 engine. The piece of flak, no bigger than the tip of your finger, was found in the engine cowling.

89

726th Bombardment Squadron over Pola Naval Base, Italy - Feb 20th, 1945.
1st Lt. Harold S. Patterson, Pilot. Lead Crew, Flight "B".
Lt. Burton Schilling, Lead Navigator
Lt. William "Dead-Eye" Bodie, Lead Bombardier.
S.Sgt. A. Kozakis, Nose Gunner, 19th mission.

INTERLUDE

AMORE SCUZÁTEMI

Upon our return from the day's mission (March 4, 1945, Graz, Austria Marshalling Yards) we completed our post-briefing and were returning to our tent when Pat, our Pilot, announced "You shall be going to Rest Camp in the morning." We rejoiced at this wonderful news. It was past due for our crew's Rest Camp assignment. I had just completed my 23rd mission (39th sortie). Usually, crews are sent to Rest Camp upon completion of 15 to 18 missions.* Many times, if a crew is shot down and returns, they have priority. At times, I thought I was "flak happy" when Rest Camp didn't come our way.

Everyone began getting ready for our trip to the Isle of Capri (Rest Camp) via Naples. We packed our B-4 bags with our Class "A" uniforms and shining dress shoes.** Man, we were past due to hit the town and shine!

The impact of going to Rest Camp was beginning to wear off when my crewmates realized they didn't have enough funds to last them during the trip. It seemed, simultaneously, they all gathered around me and my bunk. You see, I didn't smoke or drink hard liquor and I was chosen "the keeper of the booze" and of course, I had stored my cigarettes with the liquor. My musette bag contained 10 cartons of

---

* Our Group and Squadron used the following system for crediting the aircrews' missions and sorties. If the crew flew beyond a specific radius of action, it was credited with 2 sorties and still one mission (take off, bombing the target, and returning to your base). Two sorties were credited to the crew member when the target was located beyond the specific radius of action:

i.e. Vienna, Austria credit: 1 mission-2 sorties

Northern Italy credit: 1 mission - 1 sortie

My tour of duty was completed when I flew 35 missions (54 sorties). My combat flying times completed was 260.55 combat hours. Grand total flying time was 467.30 hours.

** All air crew members were issued a B-4 bag in lieu of a G.I. barracks bag. The B-4 bag is similar to today's two-suit Samsonite bag with an exterior zipper packet (full size) on one side of the bag and two exterior zipper pockets on the opposite side. The bag had a leather mid section (top) with a leather handle and a full zipper for opening the bag. The interior contained three clothes hangers and a canvas cover with a strap to enclose the uniforms. This feature kept the uniform from wrinkling. One could easily carry forty pounds of personal clothing, toilet kit and shoes. The bag exterior was weather proof and water tight.

cigarettes. A bonanza for any G.I.! Need I say more? Without much bitching between us, I gave each crew member a carton of cigarettes. "Kozakis, we owe you," "Greeko, I'll make it up to you," echoed within the tent. Having a carton of cigarettes to any G.I. was like having a couple of hundred bucks in your pocket! In other words, you were "loaded." One could purchase (barter) a ticket to the opera, spend a week in a bar, or most importantly, spend a week with a girl and much more—to each his own!

The following morning, "happy as a bird on a turd," we, the crew enlisted men, were at the edge of the runway waiting for the B-25 that would fly us to Naples. After an anxious hour or two, the aircraft arrived and the Major (Pilot) gave us a pep talk (how to behave and to stay out of trouble) with his final words, "I will personally pick you up within a two week period and do not hitch a ride back to the base." The message was loud and clear, we all concurred!

The plane ride (a B-25 twin engine medium bomber) was short, bumpy and noisy. Now, I'm sure, I'd rather fly in the B-24 (a 4 engine heavy bomber) and I was pleased I was assigned to the Liberator.

We landed without incident and the Major's final words echoed, "Remember, I'll personally pick you up for your return flight to Base Headquarters."

On our trip to our billet, we drove through the area of the city that was devastated by the war. Hardly a building was spared from the bombings a year earlier. Some of the buildings were complete rubble, where many others had their shell blown off and the floors and interior walls remained. I wondered, where and how do the people survive in this environment? We quickly learned why many say "War is hell."

Upon arriving to our quarters, the desk sergeant informed us we would billet here for 2 or 3 days prior to our trip to the Isle of Capri. It didn't make any difference to us: We were not flying combat and our time was our own!

The billet is a requisitioned and renovated three story apartment building. We select our rooms and store our belongings for safe keeping and make ready for a walk into the city.

The six of us head for the nearest plaza, an open area with stores, bars, and people. In no time, a photographer approaches us for photos. We oblige after agreeing on the price, paid by three cigarettes each.

Rodriquez suggests we have a drink as he leads us to a small bar, down a few steps and into what was once somebody's cellar. I don't drink alcoholic beverages, but not to spoil the camaraderie, I select a small glass of vino. For this action, my crewmates call me "Titty Baby." They drink cognac and brandy. Ugh!

Time passes while you're having fun and at this juncture we paired off to find our adventure. I with Balzer, O'Laughlin with Realley, and Rodriguez with Carrington took off in three different directions.

Balzer and I were strolling along the breakers at the waterfront overlooking the Bay of Naples. Suddenly, I feel a tug on my arm. There stands a young boy about ten-to-twelve years old asking if we want a "girl." Can you imagine our surprise? A twelve-year-old pimp? At first I hesitated and Lauren assured me we wouldn't get into any trouble. "Remember the Major," I said to myself. Lauren persisted and we followed this boy for about 30 minutes and about ten blocks distance where we came upon an open court with apartment buildings on all sides. Lauren followed the boy to one of the apartments as I rested on a nearby bench in the courtyard. Children were playing about while an old lady, like a mother hen, was watching her flock.

It was not long thereafter a young lady (approximately 25 to 28 years old) sat down beside me. Her black shining hair was neatly combed, no facial make-up was visible and her dress neat and clean reminded me of a typical young lady back home.

After introducing ourselves, we conversed for about 30 to 40 minutes and in English she explained, she came to pick up her daughter, as it was close to suppertime. She asked if I would join them and her mother for supper. I, without giving it a second thought, obliged. A home cooked meal ran through my mind! As the three of us began to leave the courtyard, the young boy arrived and informed me that Lauren would stay with him and he would contact me later. The young boy recognized the lady and they spoke in their native tongue for a minute or two. Thereafter, I followed Maria, the young lady, and Gina, her daughter, to their apartment where her mother was waiting.

Their apartment was on the second floor with a spiral staircase leading to the front door. As I looked across the courtyard, I could see heavy bomb damage of the nearby buildings. The apartment next door was almost destroyed with all its exterior walls missing. Maria cautioned me not to open any doors and walk into the room. The floors may be gone and a hazardous fall would follow. I stayed close to Maria and Gina, holding their hands for safe assurance. My thoughts and questions ran through me, "Maybe I should not have accepted Maria's invitation; why didn't I go with Lauren?" Before I could answer to myself, we were at the open front door and Maria's mother, Angelina, was waiting with an inviting smile.

She was an elderly woman with peppered grey hair, well groomed with a chignon on the back of her head, and a laced black shawl over her shoulders. She looked straight into my eyes, extended her hand as I held hers and introduced myself. Her hands were warm and soft, her

olive complexion and dark shining eyes made me feel at ease. "Maria resembles her mother," I said to myself.

Maria explained to her mother how we met and she had invited me for supper. Angelina, her mother, with a warm and charming smile was pleased and responded, "It is home when having a man around the casa." Later that evening I learned Maria's father was a prisoner of war in North Africa and her husband was killed during the African campaign.

The apartment was well furnished, drapes over the windows, carpets spread over the living room marble floor and furniture built to withstand a lifetime. I'm sure at one time this was an affluent household.

Supper was warm, nourishing, well-balanced, consisting of spaghetti with tomato sauce, cheese and olives; tea and a semi-sweet cake followed. Maria explained the cake was an Italian traditional desert called "panettone" with raisins and orange peel. It was delicious and the hospitality was most humbly accepted and appreciated.

Angelina, Maria's mother, was extremely pleased with my presence. I felt some guilt because her husband was not home. She held my hand as we conversed for some time. I, with my broken Italian, sparse Greek phrases and Yankee English, managed to communicate rather well. During our conversation, Maria prepared Gina for bed. Then I realized it was getting late and Lauren's boy did not call for me.

Angelina suggested it would be safer for me to stay for the night as it was dark outside and night was upon us. Maria concurred and explained to me it was not safe to be out at night. I cautiously accepted the invitation.

Supper was a complete delight and I volunteered to assist in the clean-up, but they would have none of that. They guided me to the couch and commanded me to relax. Without further resistance, I obeyed. Greek customs are so much like Italian customs. "The kitchen is off limits for the man." I said to myself.

The cleaning chores were completed and Angelina came to my side, grasped my hand, momentarily held it tight, and thanked me for my presence. "It has been so long since a man was home," Maria explained to me. Angelina bid us goodnight and went to bed with Gina.

Maria and I sat on the couch and we conversed and learned about each other for a long time. Her English was extremely good with her Italian accent. She was an interpreter for the British Constabulary stationed in Naples. Her father had taught her English and managed to send her to a private school where English was one of her major subjects. (The language barrier was non-existent).

I explain my trip to Capri via Naples is our route to rest camp, and I have completed 23 missions with 12 more to complete my tour of duty? We both know time is not our own. Loneliness hangs over our shoulders: the one thing we have in common. Just holding her hand and she grasping mine is the overture of a warm and amorous encounter.

Maria's arms wrapping around my shoulders encourage me to respond in a similar manner. As our cheeks meet, a warm tear moistened my cheek. We caress and kiss passionately. I, a young, lonely G.I. who has not tasted the fruits of life and she a lonely young, lovely widow, have our brief encounter. We are aware of the desire that leads us to hold onto this moment and we are pleased at the overwhelming passion that answers our two lonely hearts.

Too soon, the morning sunrise splashes the room with its warm and bright tenderness. My first instinct was how I am going to explain to Maria's mother my actions during the night. I hurriedly dress and meet Angelina in the parlor. There she smiles and hands me a cup of tea. It was apparent to me that my stay is welcomed and no explanation of my actions is required.

Angelina, Maria and I sit in the parlor watching Gina play on the carpeted floor. It is a comfortable and warm feeling we share. Maria, holding my hand, knows my life is not my own and the Army dictates my future. We both feel my departure is inevitable.

She knows my thoughts and I know hers. Loneliness vanished in the love we shared and the moment of desire that brought us together. I leave with a heavy heart and will always cherish Maria and Angelina's kindness. Life is difficult and uncertain. I wish I could stay with Maria, forget my trip to Capri. Our encounter has allowed me to experience the grace of human warmth and intimacy that can break through even the hardness and hell of flying combat.

REST CAMP ON THE ISLE OF CAPRI

Morning came sooner than our bodies and minds expected. We hurriedly dressed and prepared for our ferry boat ride to the Island. Every one was eager and enthusiastically anticipating several days of leisure living. We all had our personal adventures during the past three days without getting into mischief as the major advised us. Even though my feelings were still lingering with Maria, I accepted the fact that I would not see her again. It's tough!

Arriving at dockside, we found approximately 60 to 80 other G.I.'s and several Nurses anxiously awaiting the same ferry boat. We didn't wait long (approximately 30 minutes) when the ferry arrived. The Sergeant in charge called everyone to attention and gave us our orders and procedures to follow. There was no particular formation boarding and seating on the vessel. In an orderly and leisurely manner we all managed to seat ourselves comfortably.

I was sitting next to another gunner from a B-25 Bomb group. A B-25 is a twin engine medium bomber, mostly used on tactical bombing missions; whereas the B-24, heavy bomber, has four engines and is used on strategic bombing missions in the European Theater of Operations. My fellow gunner had red hair, a freckled complexion, was about 5'6" tall and weighed about 120 pounds. After our casual introduction, with sincerity he was explaining his dilemma. His problem was that he could not keep his lower legs warm during a flight; he wanted a pair of pants that had knitted cuff bottoms. The knitted ankle bottoms would keep his legs warm by not allowing the cold air run up his pant legs. My flight gear was made for extremely cold temperatures (-30 F to-60 F) and were not designed to solve his problem.

Like a lighting strike, I remembered visiting Lauren in the hospital. The nurses wore pants with knitted cuff bottoms, a perfect resolution for "Red's" dilemma. I explained to "Red" my recommendation and he enthusiastically concurred.

Three rows in front of us sat four Nurses. "Red," I nudged him, "now is your chance to get your pants." He looked at me like I'm flak happy and explained that he's extremely shy and bashful and can never approach the nurses. To make a long story short, I agree to help this shy G.I. Nonchalantly, I stroll by the nurses a couple of times, observing and selecting the Nurse that fits Red's height and approximate weight. Stepping in front of the nurse, I introduce myself to her. She's a lieutenant. She wears two hash bars on her sleeve telling me that she has been overseas for at least one year or more. I don't want the nurse to think I was a wise guy or being facetious. With deep concern and a humble desire to help my fellow G.I., I explain Red's problem, asking if she would sell him a pair of her pants. This sudden encounter catches her by surprise as amusing. She seems to think for a minute that I'm joking or maybe this G.I. is trying to fraternize with an Officer. (Enlisted men DO NOT fraternizes with officers.)

She takes a long meticulous look at me and I simultaneously point to Red. He's standing, observing our encounter. The lieutenant readily surmised I'm not a wise guy, but a very serious person doing a fellow G.I. a favor. Within a minute or two the nurse opens her B-4 bag and takes out a pair of trousers with knitted cuffs and hands them to me. I enthusiastically thank her, grasping her hand firmly and asking, "How much do you want for the pants?" A broad and warm smile lighting up her angelic face tells me, "There would be no charge." She motions Red to come forward and retrieve the trousers. Red hurriedly comes and sheepishly stands there for a moment before he profusely thanks the Nurse. She has a warm smile for both of us, and I can sense the pleasure she takes, giving and receiving.

The sad fact of this encounter is that I did not remember the names of the Gunner or the Nurse, and of course, we never met again. When the ferry boat docked, we embarked and went our separate ways.

I'm sure in everybody's lifetime; one has an opportunity to help his fellow man, even though you know little about the person. You just know that it is the right thing to do.

We, our crew, gather our B-4 bags and walk to the dockside and we are directed to the funicular a distance of approximately two short blocks from the dockside. There I'm looking into the sky, the solid limestone mountain stares down towards me as if to say, "climb me if you can, I dare you." It's overwhelming to say the least. We seat ourselves into the enclosed cab of the funicular. Three of us and our B-4 bags fill the cab. There are several cabs that make up the funicular assembly. We make our ascent to the top and exit into the city center about 500 feet above sea level. The Piazzetta, Umberto 1 Square, with its Bell Tower, Palazzo Cerio, municipal offices, police station and banks. The streets feathering outward like spokes on a bicycle wheel are very narrow, no wider than a donkey cart, made of cobble stones highly polished from the wear of the populace.

We are directed by the Sergeant and his two Red Cross girl assistants to the Quisisana Hotel, our billet, for the duration of our stay on the Isle of Capri. We are located down the hill known as Via Victore' Emanuel just south of the Piazzetta about one short block. The hotel was originally built as a Sanitarium in 1845 by a Scottish Doctor, George Clark, and in later years during the turn of the century, it became a four story hotel.*

---

* This present day it is the only five star hotel on the Island, known as the Grand Hotel Quisisana.

The Army Air Force requisitioned the other two hotels and one located in Ana Capri for our Rest Camp Facilities. A dozen plus Red Cross Girls are stationed here to organize recreational activities, special events, dances, site seeing trips and etc. for the men and Nurses. Yes, there was segregation on the island, the enlisted men in one area and the officers in another. The Nurses, Red Cross girls and Officers were billeted in the Officers Area of the island. That didn't bother us much; we danced with the nurses and girls anyway.

Our crew is extremely fortunate to be billeted at the Quisisana with our room overlooking the bay below. As usual we are paired to a room, Carrington with O'Laughlin, Realley with Rodriguez and Balzer with Kozakis. I couldn't believe the luxury bestowed upon us. We had not seen a room with two real beds, with springs, a thick mattress, sheets, pillows and a head board, a bedside console, with a lamp and buttons for calling room services. Living in a tent with five crewmates and having a cot to sleep in for the past six months, this sudden contrast, made our room into "heaven on earth." Without hesitation I dove on the bed adjacent to the window that I would occupy. Balzer took the other bed without bitching. Usually he bitches about everything.

On the headboard of each bed a plaque with directions of Do's and Don'ts written in bold letters, i.e., No drinking alcoholic beverages in the room, No boisterous noise (other guests may be sleeping), etc., etc. It also noted that there is No Dress Code; therefore, we can wear anything we want when we want to. However, at Dinner Service (suppertime) we shall wear our Class "A" uniforms. Our time was our own and if I wish to sleep until 0900 hrs. ; Nobody will awaken me at 0300 hrs.

After digesting my new environment and discussing with my crewmates the luxury bestowed upon us, we decided to see the island.

This friendly atmosphere abounds with multiple kiosks, quaint shops (perfume), and people walking slowly with smiles on their faces, and girls neatly dressed and men giving us a friendly wave. Not like an atmosphere of war torn Foggia.

Yes, this is really rest camp. No M.P.'s. (Military Police) patrolling the streets, no guns in place on the island, no sign of military movement, the leisure atmosphere is just like being back in my home town.

It's time for our first formal dinner, the evening meal. I hurried, shower and dress into my class "A" uniform. My low cut shoes, polished and shining, look impressive since I have worn them briefly in Naples and not during the past six months, they feel very light on my feet. Balzer and I are ready and we (the crew) meet in the corridor adjacent to our rooms. The six of us, slowly walk to the dining room located on the second floor. Approaching the entrance of the dining room, I can hear soft melodic music. As I entered, the euphony of a string quartet softly filled the air. The ambience of the room is like a Hollywood set. The tables accommodate six, making it effortless for the aircrews to break bread together. The tables have white linen, candles lighted with their soft romantic glow, china, crystal, and silverware abound. The chairs have soft cushion seats, probably requisitioned from Mussolini's palace. Two waiters to serve the guests, dressed in white jackets and black trousers stand by each table. No chow line here!! The food is excellent, cooked by the local chefs, spam when served, was camouflaged where it was unknown to the pallet. I didn't expect these kinds of accommodations, they are much more than I could imagine.

On Thursday evenings there was always a dance after the formal dinner. An excellent reason, I thought, why we wore our class "A" uniforms. The local girls and their families were invited, a good dozen or more Red Cross girls and Nurses were there also. It was a jolly good time for everyone, especially for the children that came with the local girls and their parents. Ice cream was always served at the conclusion of the dance!

Most of my leisure time was spent with my crewmates. We would walk and explore various interesting sites. Like the spectacular view from the top of the mountain in Ana Capri, where you can see the city of Sorrento jutting into the Sea of Naples. The monastery on the highest peak of Capri, where the Monks worked, and worshipped; and invited visitors for prayer, share their bread, cheese and wine. Of course, we would light a candle, say a prayer and donate a few Lira at the poor box located adjacent to the door where we exited. On the Northern Shore, at low tide, we made our way to the Blue Grotto (Grotta Azzurra) a cave carved out of a rock formation with the sea as the floor. Beautiful shades of blue and purple are reflected from the daylight entering the cave at low tide. On the Southern tip of the island from the city center, about a 40 minute walk, we visited the promenade of the Belvedere di Tuoro with a panorama view of the Faraglioni (Rock of the Sirens) an impressive rocky colossus jutting out of the sea. Beautiful gardens and handsome villas abound in the peaceful area. Just west along the coastline rocky spurs and sandy inlets continue until we reached the Enlisted Men's Pier and Beach.* A rocky area with fingers of sand to slumber on during a warm sunny March afternoon. A short distance away, 20 minutes, we explored the Krupp Walk, built by a German philanthropist, a small ancient road located at the bottom edge of a cliff rising 1000 feet plus or minus a few feet. It's a 20 minute walk down along side of the cliff and a 45 minute walk up the side of the cliff. We walked this area only once!!

The St. Valentino House is a beautiful villa with interior floors of various shades of marble and the interior walls made with mirror finish (glass) from the floors to the ceilings. At the house, the Red Cross Girls encouraged us to relax on the comfortable lounges, read magazines, play checkers, play ping pong and cards (NO gambling). Most importantly, the Girls served ice cream every afternoon. It became our favorite hide-away!!

Once in a while I would stroll alone, away from the hotel and ponder if I would complete my tour of duty. I was told that if I completed 15 missions, my odds to complete my tour would be favorable. Well, I just completed my 23rd mission and I felt

---

* Between 1950 and 1960, the Enlisted Men's Pier and Beach became the Marina Piccola, the favored beach of the local jet set.

certain I would be home by the end of spring time. On this particular morning, the sun was shining and a cool brisk breeze was flowing from the sea. I stopped at a Kiosk and purchased a sleeveless sweater with red and white horizontal stripes. Heck there is no dress code, so I instantly wore it over my khaki shirt. The warm feeling over my chest was most inviting. My walk along the inclined plain continued, at approximately 25 yards up the incline I could see several Officers approaching me. The closer they came I recognized that they were Infantry Officers because they wore Eisenhower jackets and combat boots. Most importantly, the leader of the group was a 3 star General; he was slim, about 6ft.3in.tall, and wore a 5th Army patch on his left shoulder. Instantly I froze at attention, me with my red and white striped sweater, and waited for the Officers to pass. General Mark Clark was approximately 10 ft. away and called to me, "Be at ease sergeant and come forward." I executed his command without hesitation while he asked me a few questions. "Sergeant, do you like Capri for a rest camp and why?" I answered the General affirmatively and explained my feelings and opinion of Capri. He and his Officers listened to me extol the virtues of the island and emphasized the non-existence of military equipment or movement which made this island environment a perfect place for a Rest Camp. Then the General, thanking me for my opinion, told me the Army was planning to build a rest camp on Ana Capri for the Enlisted Men. Little did we know then the War in Europe would end victoriously for the Allies in May.

They continued their walk down the incline road and I continued my walk up the incline road. My stroll quickly became a fast walk back to the hotel for lunch and to tell my crewmates of my encounter with General Mark Clark and his Staff. They would not believe a word I told them. Oh well, c'est le guerre !!

It was two days later and slowly walking along the narrow streets looking for a shop that sold the Good—Luck Capri Bell, a silver bell with a short silver chain that many of the air crews that visited Capri purchased and attached on the left collar of their A-2 jacket. One of the flamboyant styles of dress of the air crews was readily seen during my tour of duty. I was walking around the center of town for an hour or two without success. Returning to my hotel and a half a block away, I noticed a fancy jewelry shop on Via Victor Emanuel. Eureka!! I found the shop[*] and purchased two bells.

---

[*] It was in the month of October, 1997, 52 years since I spent my rest camp days on the Isle of Capri. I returned with my brother John so he could experience the beautiful places of the island as I did in 1945. I also had a twofold mission, unknown to John, to purchase the Good-Luck Bell of Capri. We stayed at the same hotel I was billeted in 1945 today known as the Grand Hotel Quisisana, the only five star hotel on the island.

Many grand changes have been made over the years past and today the streets are wide enough for busses to pass except in the inner city where donkey cart roads still exist with their polished cobble stones. The kiosks and quaint shops remain; La Piazzetta is still the center attraction of the island. The fancy jewelry shop is at the same location only the front facade is elaborately finished and called "Alberto e Lina Jewelry".

It is a cool sunny morning, also my 74th birthday. It reminds me of my 21st birthday sleeping under an olive tree during my first night in Italy, 1944. I hurry, walking to the jewelry store to purchase the bell I wanted. The young lady, about 40 years young, greets me and without hesitation I draw out from my pocket a photo of the bell. Showing it to the lady, "Do you have this bell? "She took one look at the photo and called in a shrieking voice, "Mama, Mama, Mama!!" I was startled and froze where I was standing. Within a few seconds an old lady with grey hair and a black shawl over her shoulders enters the room assisted by her cane. The young lady (store keeper) thrusts the photo to her mother. She holds the photo gently, not to bend it and absorbs its content, A few seconds pass, maybe a minute or so, and I see tears rolling down the cheeks of the lovable elderly lady. Gaining their composure they tell me and explain their reactions when they saw the photo of the bell. The elderly lady is Mrs. Alberto E Lina and the young lady is her daughter. During the war Mrs. Alberto, as a young girl, designed and made the bells. The present bell is still made of silver with the chain, only the shape of the bell differs slightly. I purchased two bells and Mrs. Alberto gave me two more bells. A most gracious gesture, I thought, in return I gave them the photo of the original bell. WE were all pleased with this morning's encounter. We talked together for about an hour and in that time Mrs. Alberto thanked me for the photo and I reciprocated, she began to tell me the story of the bell, the real story and the legend. They are as follows:

THE REAL STORY OF THE GOOD-LUCK CAPRI BELL

Our company produced the precious copy of St. Michael's silver bell that was given as a gift from the Isle of Capri to President Truman during the Second World War. The bell arrived on President Truman's desk few minutes before the announcement of Germany to surrender and it happened to be the first bell in the world ringing the end of the war. This first precious copy is now kept with President Truman's memorabilia in the U.S.A. National Archives.

THE LEGEND OF THE GOOD-LUCK CAPRI BELL

An old Capri legend tells the story of a shepherd boy, who lost his sheep on the way back home in the evening. That sheep was his only possession, because he was very poor and lived with his mother in a hut. The boy stood there in the dusk crying, when he thought he heard a faint ringing in the distance. He rushed off in that direction, thinking it was the sound of his little sheep's bell, but when he reached the edge of the gorge a sudden light appeared to him; it was St. Michael, who hung around his neck a little bell, saying it would save him and his mother from every harm. Since that day, his life was filled with the light of charity and happiness, and on the site of the Apparition, a villa called St. Michael was built. The little bell, reproduced for you in a silver or gold good-luck charm, will be your talisman of fortune and success.

Our days on Capri are ending and it's time to leave and make our room for a new crop of men to enjoy their Rest Camp. I certainly was fond of the most comfortable bed and the cuisine was delicious. I also knew we had to return to our base so we can earn our keep. Time waits for no one and the ferry boat does not wait for us. We hurried, getting into the ferry and Naples is but an hour away. Upon our arrival to Naples the boys manage to hitch a ride to the airfield, I plan to stay at the billet for a day. My mind is with Maria, maybe I can find her I told my crewmates. They responded with," Kozakis, Greek, you are crazy, remember what the Major told us." I answered. "I'll be with you guys in a couple of days." I must confess my thoughts were with her during my stay on the isle of Capri.

First, I walked down by the bay where Balzer and I met the young boy, no boy! Then I tried to follow the routing that Balzer, the boy and I took two weeks earlier, again no success. You guessed it I was lost! After a couple of hours of dismal failure to find Maria, I knew I would never see Maria, Angelina and Gina again.

Downhearted I returned to my billet, gathered my B-4 bag and the Sergeant drove me to the airport. My crewmate succeeded to fly back to our base. Today was not one of my better days. I have been waiting for approximately two hours, no aircraft arrived. Also anxiously waiting for a flight to Foggia are four Lieutenants, all fighter pilots from the 84th Fighter Group. Their home base is located north of Foggia. Castilluccio, my base, is 21 kilometers south of Foggia. We waited and waited until I saw a truck parked nearby with Foggia written on its front bumper. I ran to the driver of the truck, and explained our predicament, he motioned us to hop on board and our drive to Foggia began. Lucky, yes but the 6 to 7 hour ride on the back of the truck was most uncomfortable to say the least. Many of the roads taken by the driver are not paved and we bounced around like ping pong balls, our butts were sore from the pounding they received.

We arrived in Foggia at about 2300 hours. We said our "good byes" and thanked the driver for his kindness. The Lieutenants went northbound I went in a southerly direction. I ran to the A A F building located a couple of blocks away in time and hitched a ride with the Courier that leaves Foggia for my base, 451st, every night at this hour. Feeling with exhilaration, I knew I was on my way home!!

Arriving at Group Headquarters, it was midnight; I thanked the Courier and began my last mile to my Squadron, home sweet home!! The shortest distance between two points is a straight line, so I was taught in school. Thus, I shall follow the telephone cables that lay on the ground surface to my Squadron. The distance is a quarter mile less than the taking roadway.

It was a fairly good moon lit night and the cables are readily seen. Within the hour I arrive at my tent, all is quiet, no one moving about. The boys are sacked out in their respective cots. I quietly undress and get into my bunk. Sleep comes quickly and I'm out like a light.

Morning rises, my crewmate see Kozakis in his sack. Surprise! Surprise!! They quickly wake me from my dear slumber and asking questions about my return. How?

When? Where? I respond with answers that satisfy their curiosity. It's time for breakfast and time to fly again the honeymoon is over, we have to earn our keep! Two days pass and we are flying to Brux, Austria, our mission is to destroy the Marshaling Yards that the enemy uses to ship supplies to their troops. Everything is back to normal for our crew. C 'est le guerre!!

U. S. A.

AIR FORCES REST CENTER

BENE ET BONUM VOBIS
OMNES· SCIANT HOC SCRIPTO

s/sgt *Achilles Kosaris*

INSVLAM CAPREÂM VISITAVIT ET MEMORIA ILLIVS
PVLCHRITVDINIS ATQVE MAGNIFICENTIAE VITAM PERMANEBIT

LT· GENERAL IRA C. EAKER

WITNESS MY HAND
LT· COLONEL, AIR CORPS

CAPRI, ITALY
ANNO DOMINI 1945

W. O Laughlin   G. Really Jr.   A. Kozakis   L. Balzer

W. Carrington   A. Kozakis

Naples Mar. "45 enroute to Rest Camp—Isle of Capri"

CAPRI · Umberto 1 Square –
Foreground Palazzo Cerio

La Campanina
Good - Luck
Capri Bell

CAPRI · Marina Piccola (small
harbor) and the "Faraglioni"

The bell

ENLISTED MEN'S PIER AT CAPRI 1944-1945
(SMALL HARBOR) THE "FARAGLIONI" IN THE BACKGROUND

TODAY'S LOCAL JET-SET "MARINA-PICCOLA"

THE FARAGLIONI

THE REST OF
THE STORIES

THE PO VALLEY

The winter of 1944/1945 stalemate along the German Gothic Line, south of the Apennine Mountains of northern Italy, made living conditions for the American 5th Army and the British 8th Army, at times, most unbearable. It was the coldest and wettest winter during the past 60 years. Heavy equipment, trucks and artillery, could not be moved in the quagmire of mud. Many times pack mules were used to carry supplies to the troops entrenched on the mountain side and in caves that were found by a lucky few. The weak "Under Belly" of Italy, as Prime Minister Churchill called it, was no picnic. It was a long and bloody campaign that cost more lives lost and wounded of the Infantry soldiers than any other campaign in western European Theater of Operations.

Many readers, I'm sure, are not familiar with the Po Valley spring offensive located in the heart of northern Italy. Brilliant planning by the Mediterranean Allied Air Forces (MAAF) deprived the Axis forces from receiving reinforcements of material, ammunition and men to wage war. I believe it began as far back as February 20, 1945, when we, the 451st Bombardment Group, bombed and destroyed the German naval base located in Pula, Northern Italy. The cohesive strategy of bombing the enemy marshaling yards and bridges leading into northern Italy from Austria were successful in many areas during the months of February and March. The successful bombing greatly disrupted civilian and military supplies from reaching their intended destinations. My missions completed between January 5 and April 5, 1945, were concentrated on marshaling yards at 64% and petrochemical plants at 28.5%, including a two week Rest Camp period for our crew from March 5 to March 19, 1945.

The bad weather of January 1945 grounded the 15th AAF for 83% of the month. It was so bad, our Group flew only five missions and I managed to fly on two of them (January 5 to Zagreb, Yugoslavia rail installations and January 20 to Linz, Austria, marshaling yards).

The Po Valley Spring Offensive commences on April 9, 1945, when the 15th AAF began their massive bombardment of the German fortifications and troop concentrations along the Santorno River and vicinity of Lugo with direct support of the British 8th Army. The American 5th Army under the command of General Lucian K. Truscott Jr. was stalled because of bad weather.

The bomber crews selected are the cream of the crop that have performed their tasks successfully and proven to succeed in air combat. Precision timing, skillful and accurate navigation and bombing are paramount. This was not an ordinary briefing, top secrecy was pledged by all crew members flying today's mission. After studying the maps and photographs of our bombing sector of the German front lines, we are dismissed and reminded that we cannot discuss the mission once we leave the briefing room. Most importantly, we cannot tell our ground crews where we are going as we usually do. Harsh words from my ground crew made it difficult for me to respond to their questions.

Today's bomb load consists of clusters of antipersonnel fragmentation bombs (frags). Personally, I detest bombing with frags because they are made up into a cluster of several bombs. When the clusters are dropped from the aircraft and hit the air stream and prop wash of other air craft, the cluster breaks apart and momentarily the frags flutter about in all directions until they begin their descent to the intended target. During these initial few seconds an aircraft not in its proper position of flight can easily be blown apart by the frags.

This is a tactical and not a strategic bombing mission, no mistakes can be tolerated. Timing to bomb our objective is paramount. The heavy bombers of the 15th AAF are given one-and-one-half hours to complete the mission over the target area. It is the main weight of the attack with 825 heavy bombers. Also flying on the same mission, are 234 medium bombers and 740 fighter bombers. The sky is full of Allied aircraft. Every direction I turn my turret, aircraft are easily visible and I have the best seat in the house to watch the show.

Our Group is assigned to bomb Apple Section of the German front lines where heavy concentrations of troop movement are located. Today our bombing altitude is 18,000 to 20,000 feet, much lower than our normal bombing altitude of 24,000 to 25,000 feet. We reach the IP of the bomb run and below me at 12 o'clock I see the white arrow (1/4 mile long x 1/10th mile wide) pointing directly to the Axis lines, also, I see at approximately 12,000 feet altitude colored (red, yellow, blue and white) anti-aircraft bursts directly over the German troop concentration, directing our bombardiers where to drop our frags to the enemy below. We don't want friendly fire to hit our troops. Our bombs hit our intended target with excellent results. The mission lasted five-and-one-half hours without any mishaps. This was a milk run for our crew.

On the 10th of April (D+2) the same crews and procedures are followed to bomb "Baker" Section of the Axis lines with 648 heavy bombers in close coordinated support with the British 8th Army. The weather is C A V U. It is another milk run for the 451st Bombardment Group. I'm sorry to relate, it was no milk run for Lt. Gilson and his crew of the 464th Bomb Group, 779th Bomb Squadron that followed our Group over the target area. Their aircraft received a direct hit in between number one and number two engines, folding the wing to break off. All men were killed except the Mickey Operator (Radar) who was blown from the aircraft and survived. This mission flying time was four hours and forty five minutes long. I never know if I have a milk run until I land safely at my home base. All it takes is one direct flak burst and it's no milk run for the crew on board. C'est le guerre !!

Every good weather flying day in the month of April, the MAAF is flying and destroying bridges, Axis fortifications and troops. The American 5th Army and the

British 8th Army accomplished the destruction of the Axis Forces in ten days after the break through of the front lines. The Allied Air Forces left no bridges intact for the fleeting German troops to escape. The Brenner Pass escape route to Austria is sealed off by General Truscott's 5th Army. The British 8th Army breaks out into the Po Valley and launches a high speed armored attack on flat terrain and excellent roads; no more fighting from ridge line-to-ridge line. Tens of thousands of Axis troops are captured because allied air power and the tenacity of the fighting ground troops overwhelmed the enemy. The German Generals defied Hitler's orders to scorch the countryside and northern Italy industrial installations. There is no escape route available for the Axis army.

The Po Valley offensive climaxed the long and bloody Italian campaign, the war in Italy has come to a victorious end for the Allies. It was truly a multinational force made up of and not limited to the following:

Brazilian Expeditionary Forces and 6th South African Armored Division, Units of the Ground and Air; Jewish Infantry Brigade, French and Greek Brigades: Polish, New Zealand and Indian Corps; Free Italian Legnano Corps and Partisans;

The American Infantry Divisions: 34th, 85th, 88th, 91st, 92nd, 10th Mountain, 442nd Japanese American Regiment and the 1st Armored Division; The US 1V Corps West and the U S 11 Corps East.

The British 8th Army had multiple thousands of men from the colonies and British Isles.

SPECIAL ORDER OF THE DAY

Soldiers, Sailors and Airmen of the Allied Forces in the Mediterranean Theatre

After nearly two years of hard and continuous fighting which started in Sicily in the summer of 1943, you stand today as the victors of the Italian Campaign.

You have won a victory which has ended in the complete and utter rout of the German armed forces in the Mediterranean. By clearing Italy of the last Nazi aggressor, you have liberated a country of over 40,000,000 people.

Today the remnants of a once proud Army have laid down their arms to you—close on a million men with all their arms, equipment and impedimenta.

You may well be proud of this great and victorious campaign which will long live in history as one of the greatest and most successful ever waged.

No praise is high enough for you sailors, soldiers, airmen and workers of the United Forces in Italy for your magnificent triumph.

My gratitude to you and my admiration is unbounded and only equalled by the pride which is mine in being your Commander-in-Chief.

H. R. Alexander

Field-Marshal,
Supreme Allied Commander,
Mediterranean Theatre.

MAGIC 35

The month of April 1945 was the busiest, most varied and exciting month of my tour of duty. I flew on twelve missions and received credit for ten. On two missions we returned with our bombs because of the 10/10 under cast, therefore, no credit—just a ride in the blue yonder.

We, our crew, flew on the second day of the month with devastating results bombing the Marshaling Yards at St. Polten, Austria. The enemy yards were destroyed beyond description.

On the fifth, we were bombing the Marshaling Yards at Brescia, Italy, with similar results, curtailing supplies that were being shipped to the German troops in northern Italy.

On April 7 and 8, cloud cover over the target areas prevented us from bombing our assigned targets. We returned with our bombs. To my regret, no mission was credited for either day.

The ninth and tenth, only the best-of-the-best crews of the 451st Bomb Group flew the missions. They are very important dates in the annals of WWII. Remember, the Po Valley.

On April 19, 20, 21, 23, and 24, we flew all tactical bombing missions supporting the U S 5th Army and the British 8th Army with outstanding results. On the twentieth we completed the only undisputed perfect mission in the entire European Theater of Operations. Thirty-seven heavy bombers of the 451st Bomb Group, each with six 1000 pound RDX bombs, destroyed the Lucia Road Bridge. Timing and perfect formation of the aircraft and crew was a most critical factor for a successful mission.

On any given day during our blitz on German troops and their fortifications, especially at this juncture of the war, over 1200 Allied aircraft were in the air offensive. At times it was like a three ring circus. As I observe below me at 2 o'clock while on our way to our target located in the Brenner Pass, a Brazilian Squadron of P-47 fighter bombers with two 500 pound bombs, one under each wing, are bombing a bridge. Each aircraft peeling off the formation would bomb the bridge until it was destroyed. Wow! This is better than a movie.

In a span of 22 days, our crew flew strategic and tactical missions. Other crews were ferrying American prisoners-of-war back to Italy from their internment camps. Most satisfying and important for the war effort, we were running out of strategic targets because of the Allied advances on all fronts. The Allies had superiority of the air and at last it was a feeling of great exhilaration for me. No enemy fighters to worry about, just the dreadful flak and the weather.

Flak is like lightning in your midst. Crackling and tearing up the sky and any object or person in its wake. Instantly it captures your attention; there is no place to hide, no fox hole to blend into, just observe and pray it passes you by. Many times, other aircraft and crews would be hit by the menacing and dreadful flak. I would pray and ask The Almighty, "Why them and not me?" I have no answer! I just pray for their salvation.

Today, before tomorrow's mission, Pat (my pilot) came to see me. He recommended that I stand down and not to fly tomorrow's mission, and wait for a "milk run" to complete my tour of duty (35 missions or 50 sorties) that would soon follow. I respectfully responded with a firm and humble, "Thank you, Pat, but no thanks." I continued, "I trained with you, I flew with you and I'm going to complete my tour with you. That bottle of champagne is waiting for us when we fly together and I complete tomorrow's mission." Pat concurred and firmly shook my hand; he knew how I felt and I knew how he felt. That ended our meeting.

On April 25, 1945 the 727th Squadron of the 451st Bomb Group is leading our mission to bomb the Marshaling Yards at Linz, Austria. My four previous missions to Linz were always long and deadly to endure—none were milk runs. The 726th Squadron follows and the 725th, the 724th complete the formation. First Lt. E. H. Stresky, Pilot, and his crew are the last aircraft ("tail-end Charlie") in the lead flight.

Take off and assembly of the formation with the group ran smoothly, everything by the numbers. The Group was soon passing the Adriatic Sea below with all Squadrons in their proper positions. We, Pat's crew, are leading our flight and following tail-end Charlie, Stresky's aircraft, and sucking it up to make a tight formation. The weather is CAVU, no clouds to obscure my view of the tail gunner of Stresky's crew. Our aircraft and our flight are behind and slightly below their aircraft to miss their prop wash.

As usual our missions into Central Europe directed us to fly over the Alps. During this flight, it increased our altitude considerably and the German radars would always know we are approaching their territory. They have the direction and speed of our Group; thus, they alert their anti-aircraft batteries and fighter Wings. No way, we could fly low and miss their radar sites. The 8th AAF had this advantage over the 15th AAF when flying into German-held territory.

Approximately three hours pass since take off, my thoughts meander and I ask myself, "Will the German anti-aircraft batteries be tracking us today or will they have a barrage to greet us?" I answered to myself, "It all depends on the weather over the target area." If it's CAVU, they will track our Group. If the undercast obstructs their view, a barrage* will be there to greet us. Time and the weather will tell.

Our position in the flight allows me to easily watch the tail gunner of "tail end Charlie," of Lt. E. Stresky's crew. He is only 25-to-35 yards in front and slightly above me. We began a friendly exchange of waving and giving the "high sign" to each other.

---

*   A barrage of flak is made of a cube—one mile wide, one mile high and one mile long, with intense and heavy flak from 88mm, 105mm and 128mm anti-aircraft batteries.

Even though I personally didn't know him, I felt he was my buddy. We kept this friendly exchange until we reached the "I P" (Initial Point of the bomb run).

Within two minutes of the bomb run, flak began its devastating tracking of our Group. At first, two or three bursts explode in front and below our aircraft. The menacing black puffs floating by continue to multiply with intensity. The bursts ever so close, making our ship bounce like a ping pong ball. I know this is no" milk run"!!

Twenty-five or thirty-five yards in front of my turret and slightly above me, within seconds, just before I heard "Bombs Away", Lt. Stresky's aircraft receives a direct hit!! The aircraft lifts like a feather and lurches to my left for a second or two and then makes a steep banking dive to my 10 o'clock position and down it goes. I'm watching for parachutes, none are visible, except what I thought was a flak helmet falling out of the waist section of the doomed aircraft. I immediately alert my crew in our waist section and hopefully they can see parachutes. We rally off to our left and head for home. We complete our mission with very good results in the target area. Our Group lost one aircraft and another badly damaged by flak. At post briefing we told the Intelligent Officers (S2) no parachutes were seen.

Returning to our tent, jubilation for completing my tour* was not to be! All I could think was my newfound buddy, his crew are no longer with us. Rejoicing will have to wait. On the following day our Group was bombing the Marshaling Yards at Sachsenburg, Austria with excellent results. Upon return 12 men in our Squadron completed their tour of duty. Jubilation and parties for these men were being held. Finishing my tour with my crew a day earlier is extra special for me. We open and jointly drink the bottle of champagne I've been saving for this occasion. Happy hour came a day late. I'm alive and reborn knowing I shall not be flying combat missions and I'll be going home very soon. At this juncture of my tour, I was inducted into the prestigious rolls, as a life member, of "The Lucky Bastard Club."

So close and yet so far; or maybe I should say, "I was just lucky." I often think about how many broken aircraft and bodies of bomber crewmen were shot down by the enemy throughout southern and central Europe and that their bodies may never be found.

The attached letter was sent to me by Bob Karstensen, President of the 451st Bombardment Group (H) WWII, LTD. when I asked him for the disposition of Lt. E. Stresky and his crew.

451ˢᵀ Bombardment Group (H) WWII, LTD.

GROUP HEADQUARTERS   724th   725th   726th   727th Squadrons

12 October 2008

Achilles Kozakis
2225 Vogel Lane
Brookshire, TX 77423

Hi Achi,

    First off: Thanks for your continued devotion to the organization, as noted by your generous donation of $200.

    As to your request for information on the Edward H. **STRESKY** crew, this is what I have: Aircraft #44-8776 flying from the 727th Bomb Squadron

1st Lt. Edward H. Stresky, Pilot KIA - Buried at Zachary Taylor National Cemetery in Louisville, KY.
1st Lt. Arthur L. Miskend, Copilot, KIA - Buried at Ardennes American Cemetery in Neupre, Belgium.
1st Lt. James R. Gore, Navigator, POW - Was a member of our organization but died in January 1991.
Sgt. George D. Meyran, Nose Gunner, KIA - Buried at Ardennes American Cemetery in Neupre, Belgium.
T/Sgt. Ora P. Arnold, AEG, POW - Was a member of our organization but died in October 2005.
S/Sgt. Paul Hendrix, Ball Gunner, KIA - Buried at Ardennes American Cemetery in Neupre, Belgium.
Sgt. David W. Peterson, Waist Gunner, KIA - Burial location unknown.
T/Sgt. Quentin H. Thorvig, ROG, KIA - Burial location unknown.
S/Sgt. Arthur J. Barker, Tail Gunner, KIA - Buried at Zachary Taylor National Cemetery in Louisville, KY.

    Lt. Robert P. Mitchell, Navigator - gave this accounting of his eyewitness viewing:

"On 25 April 1945, I was flying in the same flight as A/C #44-8776 which was piloted by Lt. Stresky. While the formation was over Linz, Austria, and just before 'bombs away,' a burst of flak struck his ship in the bomb bays. Immediately the plane went into a steep dive and began to flame. It was apparently out of control, as it crashed into the ground and exploded. Two parachutes opened. The time was 1247."

Hope this helps .... In comradeship,

Bob K

Robert Karstensen, President / 1032 S. State St. / Marengo, IL 60152 - Ph. (815) 568-7766 / Fax (815) 568-0451

MY FIRST HOMECOMING

It was in the late spring of 1945. The war in Europe ended five weeks earlier. Perry Como was enjoying the making of his first Gold recording *"Till the end of Time"* and I was home on a well deserved furlough for the upcoming 4th of July holiday. My long awaited and happy return from combat in Europe, just like the other hundreds of thousands of G.I.'s, was the pinnacle of any spectacular dream. Only it was true!

I was home, healthy and in one piece and momentarily living on a cloud.

The greetings received were overwhelming. *"Glad to see you safely home"* came with happy and enthusiastic hand shaking or hugs and kisses that made my day over and over again; a homecoming that far exceeds the expectations of this young soldier. I'm sure I was one of the luckiest G.I.'s on earth.

On the third day, 17th of June, following my return, the day was exceptionally hot & sunny. A perfect New England day for the beach, I surmised. The two mile walk to the Lynn Beach Metropolitan District Bathhouse was short, sweet and the old landmarks en route again assured me I was really home. Nonchalantly walking to the beach I walked through the Lynn Commons (Lynn became a township in 1629) with their cast iron fences surrounding the *"village green"* and with its Fountains and Bandstand where summer concerts were played on Wednesday & Sunday evenings (weather permitting). Spectacular lighting schemes and water displays were coordinated with the music and I'm sure provoked the fantasies and imagination of all who had this marvelous opportunity to watch & listen. Nearby as I continued my stroll, I came upon an old and precious monument—St. George's Greek Orthodox Church, where as a young boy, I diligently attended. Across from the church and overlooking the commons, stands Lynn Classical High School (the school I attended and graduated from) with it's yellow brick walls and stone facade and columns from the front stair entrance to the third floor. In my mind, it was the *"Parthenon"* of West Lynn. All this and other landmarks too numerous to mention were home to me!

After checking into the bathhouse and renting a pair of swim trunks & a locker, a brief refreshing shower followed. Thence, through the tunnel below I crossed the street located above and finally on to the crystal sandy beach made of white fine grains left by the endless tides and mother nature's helpers.

Suddenly, I remembered as it came back to me like being struck by a bolt of lightning. The moment my bare feet sank into the inferno of hot, hostile, burning sand, I knew I should have worn shoes. Hopping, skipping running about, I hastily ventured for about 20 yards through this bed of fire. Finally I came upon a lonely stretched out blanket. What a relief! An island, a safe haven surrounded by the hot sands of Lynn Beach.

Pausing & rubbing my scalded feet as I sat on the blanket, I observed no one around me. I'm sure the Owner would not mind sharing this precious alleviation for a moment or two. *"Oh what the hell . . . . they can't send me back to combat"*, I muttered to myself even though I knew I was trespassing on someone's property.

Several minutes had elapsed, yet no one came to retrieve their blanket. I made myself more comfortable and as the cool New England breeze swept over my body and with the warm soft blanket beneath me, I dozed off into sweet slumber.

It must have been at least ten or twenty minutes after I fell asleep when I felt droplets of the cold Atlantic Ocean on my backside. Instantly I turned over to find myself looking up into a towel hovering over me, a wet bathing suit and a young smiling freckled face with long wet red ringlets. Momentarily, nothing was said, she just continued to dry herself. I spoke first by apologizing for the intrusion, as I explained my earlier encounter with the hot sandy beach. I started to get on my feet but she stopped me by saying *"don't get up, stay as you were"*, and she continued to dry and comb her hair.

Her name was Lenora, a pleasingly plump, green eyed, five-foot four Irish lass. Lenora knew I was in the Army having read my dog tags during my brief sleep. And within the hour, through casual conversation, we began to feel like old friends as we both knew the same people and had graduated from the same high school.

A quick swim in the cooled waters followed and the hours together passed quickly. As the evening shadows grew longer, it was time to depart.

During my remaining furlough Lenora and I enjoyed evenings out—dancing to the popular swing bands that made their one week stands at Kimball's Starlight Open Air Ballroom located in Wakefield (approximately 15 miles from Lynn.) We swam during the day and danced at night. The rest of the time was made up of doing what came naturally.

We soon found out that time waits for no one, and this rings truer for the Army. My orders had been cut, and I am commanded to report to the Commanding Officer at Atlantic City for processing and re-assignment.

I have no regrets except maybe that I had more time. My homecoming and furlough were a taste of heaven on earth for this G.I. But Atlantic City with its Boardwalk is known to be a paradise for the G.I.'s stationed there, with its sandy beaches, Steel Pier, and clubs. The Army had requisitioned the many hotels along the boardwalk for billeting the service personnel and providing a General Hospital for the wounded troops returning from the European Theater of Operations. Like a good soldier, I went willingly!

Greek Orthodox Church

Lynn Common

Lynn Classical High School

THREE DAY PASS

The days were getting shorter and the evenings slowly turned into darkness. The weather was mild and dry. Autumn was a few fallen leaves away.

Being an ambulatory patient at England General Hospital in Atlantic City during the summer and fall of 1945, I had a wonderful opportunity to enjoy a long overdue reunion with George and Ollie. The distance was relatively short. Atlantic City to Linden, NJ (their home) was only about a two-hour train ride.

Uncle George and Aunt Ollie were in their late 40's or early 50's. Happy with their lives as they were, but, having no children, they treated me and my younger brother Milton as their own. This was especially true during and after our summer vacation of 1938 when we visited them.

A three day pass would be great and relatively easy to acquire. After all, my flight surgeon was pleased to learn that I had relatives close by. I was assured this brief release from the hospital would accelerate my convalescence.

The first day and night of my 3-day pass was spent exclusively with my Aunt and Uncle. It was as if their son had returned from battle; lots of hugs, kisses, tears, laughter and reminiscing about the "old days." I'm sure they were much happier than I could have imagined.

Having arrived stateside three-and-a-half months prior to my visit and as a young soldier of 21 years, I still felt the effects of a nervous condition. By that I mean, I could not easily settle down. Most likely combat had some effect on me. But on the second evening,

I excused myself from the hospitality of George and Ollie, saying that I was going to visit an old friend whom I had met during my summer vacation in 1938. So I started out and luckily Charlie was home when I got there—on leave from the Navy. We decided to pass the evening away at a nearby bar and grill, telling each other "war stories" and mostly comparing and reviewing the past seven years. It was odd, we were so much alike, like Tom Sawyer and Huckleberry Fin. No one is a stranger!

During the course of our visit, I met a gal named Barbara—5'-3" she was pleasingly plump, with lovely blonde hair, soft & gentle hazel eyes and a smile that would take away all your fears. We danced for most of the evening and later when it was time to go home, we decided I would walk with her. So when the time came, I said goodbye to Charlie and called Aunt Ollie asking her not to wait up for me as I'd be with my old friend for a while longer.

Barbara and I were both young and lonely. The walk with her was warm and lighthearted. And when we arrived at her home—a lovely apartment nestled in a quiet, affluent neighborhood—she asked me in for coffee. We both could use some!

I followed her inside and in just a few minutes, she brought out the cups, saucers and coffee. Talking and laughing, we were learning more about each other. And I might add, I was a real gentleman. But were the truth known, my earlier intentions, my plan for the remainder of the night were not very gentlemanly, to say the least.

As my eyes surveyed the room, there on the mantle was a large beautifully framed photograph of a handsome Air Corps Captain. Shortly thereafter, I learned he was Barbara's husband of six years. He was stationed in Arizona.

Minutes turned into hours as we talked, held hands and shared intermittent soft caresses. We did not realize that the dark outside was brightening into day light.

My instincts told me that I should leave, but my emotions controlled my actions. We embraced and held tightly onto each other for what seemed an eternity, knowing all too well that this would be just a memory. A tear rolled down her soft and warm cheek touching mine. Now, not a word was spoken.

Our eyes and deep thoughts answered all questions for each of us. And at the same instant, it seemed, we both realized it would be best for all concerned, not to get emotionally or physically involved. After all, this was an innocent and brief encounter. And as fate would have it, she was leaving the following day to visit her husband in Arizona and I of course, had to return to the hospital in Atlantic City.

Exhausted by the events of the night, we lay on her bed pulling a sheet over us. Within seconds, a deep sleep overcame us and without further occurrence, slept the morning away.

Achi & Aunt Ollie 1945, Sept.

Author at age 21

SUPPLEMENT 1

AERIAL GUNNER

Gunners are the unknown members of the aircrews. I flew nine missions with crews other than my own. More often than not on these occasions, I would fly my usual position (nose turret) and only one member of the crew, the pilot, would know my name. The other crew members knew me as "the nose gunner."

Usually, we were the youngest members of the aircrew. Often, we were recent high school graduates and young men off the farm who were looking for excitement after "washing out" of the Air Corps Cadet program. Yet we were determined to fly and contribute to the war effort. We were surprisingly innocent, naïve, but not for long. We soon learned the grim reality of air combat.

Win the war as soon as possible and get on with our civilian lives—that was our goal.

Tens of thousands in this trade soon found what it was like to fly as a crew member. The air temperatures above 20,000 feet were normally 40 degrees below zero. It was necessary to wear adequate clothing and flight gear to counter the bitter cold. The flight gear was bulky and made it difficult to move about. The cramped turret positions gave little comfort during an eight hour mission.

The ball turret was the worst position on the aircraft. You were curled on your back and your knees were rubbing your ears. Try that position for an hour and you'd wish you were a waist gunner, standing and moving about the waist of the aircraft!

The tail turret, top turret, and nose turret were less cramping and accommodated movement better than the ball turret. The best of these turrets, in my opinion, was the Emerson Nose Turret. I know I'll get a lot of flak from other gunners for this opinion, but it's true.

What turret provides a head-on panorama view?

What turret allows one to sit comfortably?

What turret allows one's body to raise and lower with the twin 50 caliber machine guns?

What turret has the controls (electrical, heating system, oxygen, and turret) at a pre-positioned location above the right shoulder?

The Emerson Nose Turret!

I flew in all gun positions in the B-24 Liberator heavy bomber and found the nose turret more "user-friendly" than any other turret. Thus, the title of this book is "The Best Seat in the House."

The gunners on a moving platform (B-24 bomber) would shoot at a moving target at high speeds and at high altitudes in a most dangerous environment. The frontal enemy fighter attacks took place in milliseconds. The closure rate of speed was 500 miles per hour or more. The frontal attack would last three seconds at 800 yards to closure (200 miles per one half second). An enemy fighter diving at a formation of B-24s was nothing but a blur as it swished by the nose turret.

In gunnery school, we were taught and we mastered the cleaning and field-assemble of 50 caliber machine guns, blind folded and with gloves on. And we also learned how to maintain gun turrets. Yet we had no idea what true combat conditions were like. It was in the "school of hard knocks" that one got baptized in aerial combat.

Flak was the main concern for the bomber crews. More men and aircraft were lost because of flak than from enemy fighter aircraft. Sometimes the flak was so thick you could walk on it. And it was intense and accurate. There is no place to hide, no fox hole to dig into. You just had to sweat it out!

The 15th and 8th Army Air Forces had higher percentages of losses than any other American fighting force. The air war was not clean or safe. At times it was murderous.

The gunners and their fellow bomber crewmen were different from the rest of the Squadron personnel. They lived in a different atmosphere. The bomber crewmen reported to their Pilot (their Commander) and were insulated from the disciplinary command of the rest of the Squadron. Of course, this is true only when flying combat missions; on the ground we were treated equally with other enlisted personnel.

The relations of the enlisted crewmen with their Officers were unique in many ways. Our Pilot censored our mail, whereas the ground personnel had their mail censored by unknown Squadron officers assigned to that particular detail. Our mail was private and personal and our crewmen were like a closely knit family. We didn't require passes to go into town, Foggia. Our pilot gave us permission and that sufficed, whereas the ground crew personnel required a pass from the Operations Officer of the Squadron.

The enlisted crewmen slept in separated tents and ate in separated mess halls from the Officer crewmen. Yet in the air we were all treated equally. Each had his specific duty, and we depended on each other for our survival. This bond grew stronger with every mission. It will live within us and last a lifetime. My crewmen contributed to my survival as I did to theirs. I respect and love them all. They will always be part of my life.

Waist Position—Dressed For Combat (Winter 1944)
Courtesy of US Army

AAF combat crewman, c. 1944. This efficient outfit protected American flyers against climate and calamity. The popular Type B-15 intermediate flying jacket and A-11 trousers combination, of multilayer alpaca and wool-pile construction, was usually worn over the Type F-3 electrically heated two-piece suit, QMC wool service uniform and underwear. The electrical cord with PL-354 jack can be seen hanging down the right leg. Trousers featured thigh pockets, and the green ball of a bailout oxygen bottle can be seen in the left-leg pocket. The full-length zipper on the left leg permitted easy removal of trousers, even under water. The Type A-11 intermediate flying helmet with ANB-H-1 earphones, B-8 goggle with heated lens, and A-14 demand-oxygen mask with microphone, integrated to provide face protection from cold, wind, and flash fire. Other items of equipment included the Type B-4 "Mae West" pneumatic life vest. Hands were protected by electrically heated gloves with rayon inserts. Electrically heated shoe inserts were often worn, but QMC high-top G.I. shoes were recommended for wear under Type A-6A flying shoes shown here. The harness for the Type A-4 quick-attachable chest parachute has the Irving quick-release device. A Type C-1 sustenance vest can be seen, with the butt of a pistol in the holster under the left arm. (SI Photo A4847J)

IN THE GAME

(From the Emerson Turret)

Bombs Away! Rally left, dropping 2000 I'm heading home. Thank you dear Lord all is alright.

Ahead the vast blue engulfs my turret; cold and clear, not a cloud in sight nor a fighter to fear.

Our escorts this day are the "Red Tail Angels." The Tuskegee Airmen, making crisscross vapor trails high above our formation.

The sun's reflection, sharp and bright, bounces within my dome, and dances around me with the sparkles of light.

My eyes turn left then to the right, inspection, by observation, the wings and engines. All intact, no trailing oil or smoke. The engines are in a melodic concert, purring and humming an endless melody.

The rhythm dwells and absorbs my tired body and mind. I surrender into slumber, a reverie of peace, like a warm embrace. The sun's rays, warm and soft, comfort me again and again.

My sweat trickling down my back turns to crystals. Sensing something is amiss; I check my connections, heated suit, oxygen mask, goggles, and gloves. Nothing is wrong! It's just my instinct telling me it is time for an oxygen check.

I am alerted with a start. No time for rest the mission is half won. The major task lies ahead. Do we safely cross the dreaded Alps, do we have enough petrol? These concerns weigh heavily on my mind. Home sweet home is but a few hours away.

Many young men died too soon. For some of us more fortunate, the engines murmur on. The angels of mercy spared us this day.

Lest we forget the unfortunate heroes, there is no tomorrow. "They gave their today for our tomorrow."*

At last we pass the dreaded Alps and leave the flak towers and Luftwaffe far behind. The Adriatic is just ahead and we drop to 5000 making ready to land.

On the downwind leg our flight forms an echelon formation. Wing tip to wing tip, every air craft in its proper position is timed for landing.

---

*   written by an unknown Marine after the battle of Iwo Jima.

Touch down! The whirls of smoke from burnt rubber of the landing gear hitting the metal mat runway fills the partially opened bomb bays. Taxi to our assigned revetment, we find the ground crew "sweating out" our return.

The game is over! We blasted the Hun!

This mission is history, chalk up another one!

TOO LITTLE TOO LATE

The famine of German oil began around late August of 1944 when they lost 80% of the Ploeste oil fields and partial production of other petro-chemical plants because of heavy Allied bombings and the advancing Russian armies on the Eastern front. The continued successful Allied air attack on German petro-chemical plants, oil refiners and oil storage facilities left them with a trickle of fuel.* It was obvious that most of the German propeller-driven aircraft would not fly.

I saw first-hand an example of the enemy's lack of fuel. On April 2, 1945, we successfully bombed the St. Polten, Austrian marshaling yards. The weather was C.A.V.U. On our return routing, we flew past a German airbase and I counted 120 aircraft sitting on the ground. Presumably with empty fuel tanks for the duration.

When refineries were not producing at full capacity, The German High command knew that the war would be lost. It was a cat and mouse game during 1944, and heavily targeted during the months of November and December. The Germans repair their petrochemical facilities; we return and bomb them out of commission. That is why the battle for German oil is never an ending one.

The aviation fuel reserves of May, 1944, were 540,000 tons, in September, 1944, the fuel reserve stocks were only 180,000 tons!

The Nazi's prime defenses against our heavy bombers was flak guns (anti-aircraft artillery), flak towers, flak rail cars and flak barges

(along the Danube), heavily concentrated around their scattered German oil industry.

Vienna in June 1944 had approximately 460 guns; in December, 1944 it had 680 guns; and in February 1945 it had 800 guns and six heavily armed ghostly flak towers still remaining throughout the city. They could not be destroyed by the Germans or the Russians.) As the Russian Army advanced from the East, the Germans fortified their oil industry with more guns. Flak became the prime destructive force against our heavy bombers and their crews. We lost more aircraft and men from flak than we did from enemy fighter attacks.

Many times during the bomb run with heavy under cast (10/10) a common enemy flak attack would be a flak box *barrage*. All anti-aircraft guns (88's, 105's, and 128's) would fire at a point just short of where they assumed the bombers would release their bombs. Thus, they hoped the ensuing barrage would disrupt the bombing formation and reduce the accuracy of the mission. Of course we always flew a straight and given course without any maneuvering when we reached the I.P. (point of the bomb run) and then sweat it out until bombs away! Then we rallied off simultaneously with a sharp bank and a shallow dive to gain airspeed and quickly leave the target area. At times it was tough!

Primarily the loss of oil and shortage of trained enemy pilots brought the demise of the German air war. The Allies gained air superiority and attacked many targets without enemy fighter interception. Flak and the weather** were the only things that might stop me from completing my tour of duty at this juncture of the war.

During the month of December, 1944, there were almost 3000 new combat aircraft available for the German Luftwaffe. Among the aircraft, the ME 262 jet fighter was a dilemma for the Allied Bomber crew. It could faster and outfly our escort aircraft. Unknown to us at the time, the majority of the ME 262's were sent to the German Bomber command, whereas ten percent were sent to the Day Fighter Groups. Most of the jet-fighter pilots did not have the adequate training and flying hours. The weather hampered the success of the ME262 pilots. Most had no blind flying training and flying into and out of large cloud banks proved fatal to many young pilots.

During the latter months of the war, on a given day, the U.S.15th Army Air Force would fly maximum effort missions with more than 1200 heavy bombers attacking many targets with losses at less than one! percent. Victory was close at hand, and there was a feeling of exhilaration among us!

------

* Oil targets of the 15th Army Air Force:

"The loss of Ploeste and the destruction of refineries in Hungary has been cut deeply. Most if the remaining facilities are petroleum refineries in the Vienna area and series of synthetic oil plants ranging from Austria to Poland. Five of these synthetic plants are concentrated in Upper Silesia, two at Blechhammer and one at Odertal in Germany; one at Oswiecim in Poland, and one of minor importance at Moravska Ostrava in Czechoslovakia—all in the range of the 15th AAF. Other oil installations are at Linz, Austria and Regensburg, Germany. The greatest of all synthetic oils plants in German—controlled Europe is at Brux in the Sudetenland.

Most of these facilities have been attacked by the 15th AFF since it began to strike oil targets in the Spring of 1944. Many have been completely knocked out and subsequently repaired.

Essentially, there are five major oil refineries in the 15th AFF area of operations, producing about one-third of the gasoline used by the German armored forces and the Luftwaffe. In the six-day campaign of instrument attacks beginning December 16, all but some of the lesser refineries around Vienna were bombed.

Two of the refineries were knocked out-Blechhammer north and south; one was probably rendered inactive at Oswiecim; one is a question mark at Brux, because of bad weather; and one was missed at Odertal. (*Stars and Stripes*; Mediterranean Area Ed. Dec 26, 1944).

** The bomber aircraft were not airtight and not heated like today's aircraft. The aluminum skin of the B24 is one sixteenth of an inch thick that separated the crew from the outside environment. The wind chill temperature factor at-60 is-148 degrees. When human flesh is exposed at these temperatures, flash freezing may occur within 30 seconds. We called it *frost bite!*

Air Temperatures:	-30	-40	-50	-60
Wind Chill:	-101	-117	-133	-148

U.S. Army Research Institute of Environmental Medicine

451st Bombardment Group (Heavy) WW-IJ, Italy

B·24 Liberators of the 727th Bomb Squadron coming off the target after
bombing the Concordia Vega on Refinery at **Ploesti, Rumania** on 31 May
1944. These oil refineries were some of the highest priority targets of the
15th Army Air Forces, and the 451st Bomb Group flew 10 missions against
Ploesti (23 into Rumania) with high costs in men and aircraft before
targets were destroyed, or liberated.

Sgt. BOB HOFFMAN
RESPONSIBLE FOR PLOESTI PICTURE
Camera man on a/c *PATSY JACK* with Roland Threadgill's, 727th crew.

TID-BITS

Sixty-five years ago we were waging a bombing campaign against the industrial might of Adolf Hitler's Germany.

Today, I doubt if many people realize how young the Bomber Crews were. The crews were mostly in their late teens or early twenties between 19 to 22 years of age. My pilot, Lt. Harold S. Patterson, 28 years old, was the oldest pilot in our squadron. Similarly, our Group Commander, Col. Leroy Stefonowicz, was only 28 years old. We called him the "old man."

We were not briefed about the feelings of fear and fright during a combat mission. We didn't fly into combat cocksure we were going to come back, but we were not going to show it. We just wouldn't let our crewmates down! Our prime objective was to bring this war to a victorious conclusion and then get on with our civilian lives.

I was a young boy of 21 years with a peach-fuzz face, and I had not tasted the fruits of life. I would venture to say 80 percent of the air crews were in that category.

My first mission was a "milk run," no flak, no fighters, just bad weather en route to the target and cloud cover over the target area. The target was an enemy troop concentration around the Sarajevo, Yugoslavia, and marshaling yards. We didn't drop our bombs because of the undercast. "If flying combat missions are like this," I said to myself, "I have it made." Little did I know how combat flying would be!!

It was on my second combat mission to bomb the oil and petrochemical plants of Vienna, Austria. The weather was C.A.V.U. (Ceiling and Visibility Unlimited). Flak was heavy, intense, and accurate. I prayed and asked God Almighty to give me strength and be with me through the Hell that engulfed our squadron. When I completed that mission, I returned to my base as a young man of 21 years!

The Vienna Oil Refineries and Petrochemical Plants were located northeast of the city center, and along a four mile stretch on the banks of the Danube River. A perfect example of this is our own Houston Ship Channel, where one plant after another plant is interconnected with underground piping like spaghetti. Oh yes, the Danube was not blue as Mr. Straus wrote in his music. It was brown and it meandered through Central Europe!

A long bombing mission (flight time) would last about 8 to 8-1/2 hours, and it was vital to one's survival to wear an oxygen mask almost the entire time. Our bombing altitudes were usually 24,000 to 25,000 feet and our guns often froze when we were flying at about 16,000 to 18,000 feet. We would test-fire our guns over the Adriatic Sea en route to our target, but at a much lower altitude, say 10,000 to 13,000 feet.

We soon learned that using grooming hair oil (Brilliantine) was the best way to keep metal parts from freezing at high altitudes, whereas the government issued oil would freeze.

The aircraft were made of a bare aluminum skin riveted to an aluminum structural frame and not insulated against the high altitude freezing temperatures. Today's combat aircraft are pressurized and heated.

The high altitude temperatures were usually 30 degrees to 60 degrees below zero, and if you took off your gloves for any length of time, your hands would freeze. We called it "frost bite." If you touched the cold metal (aircraft, guns, ammunition) without gloves, your skin would instantly stick to it. That is why we were issued silk or rayon insert gloves to wear inside our regular intermediate type A-10 gloves made of goatskin and had camel hair lining with knitted wristlets that were very warm and flexible.

To overcome these extremely low temperatures at high altitudes, we were issued heating flying suits. The suits consisted of foot inserts (foot booties), pants and jacket. They were made of nylon with electrical wiring embedded in the fabric, and made to fit body tight. (You know, like some of the girls wear their blue jeans today, but not that tight!)

I would wear my electrically heated flying suit on top of my socks, T-shirt, and long underwear. Over the heating suit, I would slip into my cotton summer trousers and shirt with my Staff Sergeant Stripes and insignia sewn on the sleeves. A precaution taken in case I was shot down and became a prisoner of war (POW). The insignia was important in order to have the protection of the Geneva Convention. Then I would slip into my summer flying suit with a zipper front (easy to get into and out of) and on top of those clothes, I would wear my winter flying suit consisting of a B-10 jacket and A-9 trousers with adjustable suspenders, both lined with a soft fleece material (50/50 alpaca and wool-pile fabric) that kept out the freezing environment.

Now you have an idea why the girls, during the war, had problems finding nylon hose. The nylon was manufactured and issued to the air crews in many forms of high altitude flying clothing and parachutes.

On top of all this clothing, I wore my B-4 life vest ("Mae West"), a yellow rubber life preserver in case we parachuted or crash landed in the Adriatic Sea. Finally, I wore my parachute harness with clips to hold my chest pack parachute. The gunners wore chest pack parachutes in order to maneuver in the aircraft and fit into the designated turret. The chest pack parachute was pre-positioned adjacent to each gunner's station (turrets or waist gun) for instant use in time of need.

Our A-6 flying boots were not made for long distance walking, say over 50 yards. They were heavy, clumsy, and made with leather tops lined with lambs' wool and a zipper front. The lower section of the boots consisted of rubber soles. Our boots were warm and comfortable when worn during the mission and in the tent on cold mornings.

The oxygen masks were also heated with an electrical wiring jacket attached to the mask. The earlier issued masks would freeze at high altitudes.

All the electrical heating equipment was interconnected with snap or press-stud type connections so that one cord would be available to be connected to the turret receptacle. If you were flying in the waist position, the receptacle was located next to the gun column and the cord stretched to allow you to walk around an 8 x 8 foot area.

To relieve oneself at high altitudes, the "relief" tubes were installed at the nose section and waist section of the aircraft. However, at high altitudes, urine would instantly freeze before it left the tube. The most efficient method was to take along a bottle to handle the situation. It would be more beneficial to wait until you were flying at a lower altitude and to remember to alert the tail gunner to turn his turret far left or far right to avoid the slip stream of air from carrying the fluid into his turret. (It was one of the hazards of war for the tail gunner).

Air crew personnel usually were individualistic and sometimes flamboyant when it came to Army Air Force dress during WWII. It seems they wanted to wear something special and distinctive to separate them from other Army services. They also had the reputation as the "glamour boy" service. This image would soon fade away when we, the air crews, were under attack from German fighters and heavy flack.

The most popular garment was the A-2 flight jacket worn by the air crews. The jacket was made of seal-brown horsehide leather and lined with light brown spun silk, leather collar, zipper front, brown knitted waistband and cuffs. It was a status symbol. Especially when it was decorated with squadron, group, Air Force, and U.S.A. flag patches. The back side of the jacket was usually painted with "war art," most likely, a pin-up girl with the name of the crewman's aircraft and bombs indicating the number of missions the crewman had flown. The A-2 jacket remained the favorite garment for the air crews throughout the war and thereafter.

During the war years people were very giving and good to each other. The service men and women were treated like a kindly family everywhere we traveled in the great U.S.A.

It was a historical period that, most likely, will not be repeated. I'm proud and thankful that I was part of it.

"3-Day Pass: Visit Aunt Ollie @ Linden, NJ. Sept. 1945 (21 yrs/ old)"

The Bell of Capri

Patches worn on the A-2 Jacket L to R: 451st B.G. 726 B. Sgdn., Bell of Capri on jacket coller, 15th AAF. on left shoulder and American Flag on Right shoulder (Not Shown)

Old Patch   New Patch

A-2 Jacket w/ Patches

SCHOOL OF HARD KNOCKS

I've heard people say the "school of hard knocks" is the best teacher. Maybe so! The following example always reminds me of my younger days.

Whenever I'm extremely tired and stressed out after a grueling week of work, mentally I refer back to my days in combat.

Flying five consecutive missions, all averaging seven-and-a-half-plus hours long will really tax your mental state and physical well being. Yes, your extremely tired and stressed, knowing too well the adrenaline rush builds within you as the flak tracking your aircraft reaches out ever so closer with each successive burst that could be the very last you'll encounter! But you have a job to do and you continue with your work so that you don't let your crew members down.

What is my point? One does not *"really"* know his threshold of continuous abuse of body and mental state until one experiences it. Thus, when ever I'm extremely tired and stressed out, I think about those days in combat, then I know I can continue a bit longer under these current conditions.

TIME WAITS FOR NO ONE

My "orders" to report to my next destination are neatly enclosed in a light brown envelope with its large flap for easy access to its contents. On the top front cover, my name, rank, and serial number are easily visible for the reporting Sergeant to read. I hold the envelope protectively with my left hand and my duffle bag on my shoulder with my right hand. It holds my Olive Drab (O.D. winter) clothing issues, boots, socks, underwear, toilet kit, and a pocket Bible issued in basic training.

Proudly I wear my silver "gunner's wings," indicating I have successfully completed aerial gunnery school. Upon graduation, I also earned my first stripe P.F.C. (Private First Class) and was assigned to "flying status." Of course, these two changes to my grade and status earned me a raise in pay of approximately sixteen dollars a month. "Man, I'm loaded!" I chuckle to myself.

This is my first furlough (actually a fifteen-day delay en route to Westover Field for bomber crew transition training) after completing basic training and aerial gunnery school. At last I'm on my way home!

The train station at Laredo, Texas, is extremely small for the density of troop movements, especially when gunnery graduating classes are making their way to their destinations east, west, and north.

The hustle and bustle of troop movements are intimidating if you are not aggressive. G.I.'s with their orders in one hand and many with their duffle bags over their shoulders, some dragging them on the floor and/or holding them knee high make movement difficult and at times frustrating. The heat of the day (90 degrees) didn't help my frustration either.

My train routing to my hometown, Lynn, Massachusetts, on the North Shore, twelve miles from Boston, is via St. Louis, New York City, then Boston. This routing gives me an opportunity to visit my brother Milton who is stationed at Scott Field (St. Louis) attending radio school for the Army Air Transport Command.

Milton is two years my junior (18 years old), the baby of the family and I may add, the most handsome guy in the city. This reunion brings us together after six months absence from home. We have two wonderful days, mostly reminiscing and comparing our days from growing up with the family. It seems we take every day for granted and don't realize how precious time is until it's taken away.

As the song goes, "Time waits for no one," and my train to New York is no different. We conclude our goodbyes and I'm on my way, leaving Milton waving bye-bye, standing on the crowded platform.

I hustle and luckily maneuver a seat on the overcrowded train to New York City. It's hot and muggy. The open windows provide a cool breeze for some, but it doesn't relieve the sticky environment much. Some of the troops sack out on their duffle bags, others lean on each other, while the lucky ones like myself have a seat. At times the klickety-klack of the wheels running on the tracks lulls me to sleep.

After spending two-and-a-half days on an overcrowded train we become acquainted and friendly. Some of the G.I.'s on board come from the New England area and we spend our leisure hours bragging about our hometowns and high schools.

Arriving at and leaving from New York's Grand Central Station is no different from St. Louis—only many more people. The immense crowds hustling and bustling their way remind me of a herd of cattle in a stampede. I'm almost home. The battle is practically won. Boston is four hours away. I can relax and take it easy. As a matter of fact, I sleep all the way there.

I often wonder where the stamina and adrenalin comes from within my body to pursue my destination. The army is always "hurry up and wait." A line forms in the latrine, in the mess hall, in the P.X. (Post Exchange), in the pay line and in the train station. Name it and it's "hurry up and wait!" Time and the war wait for no one. But in the army, you learn how to wait regardless.

Visiting my younger brother Miton at Scott Field, St. Louis

DREAM

It was during this reassignment procedure that the flight surgeon told me that I should not have been on flying status. He ordered an operation on my chronic sinus condition. It was like a guy eating a sour pickle all of his life and thinking it was the sweetest pickle in the world. Luckily, I managed to complete my tour of duty and return home with out major wounds, and now I'm ordered to have an operation!

We are all patients at England General Hospital located on the Board Walk of Atlantic City, a superior facility of loving care for the wounds received during combat. The other 10%, like me, are patients admitted after our return from our 30 day furloughs and ordered to report for processing and reassignment.

The radio is softly playing and the men around our section of the ward are listening attentively. Vaughn Monroe's Orchestra and the Norton Sisters are singing "Dream," a popular tune of the present time.

As I scan the room, I can see the faces of several amputee patients with tears slowly trickling down their cheeks. The song produces a melancholy mood throughout the ward. In many ways: on the land, in the air, or on the high seas we had the same experiences enduring fear and the will to survive. The stress of combat bound us together and created the respect we have for each other. Together, we cry today, and tomorrow we will laugh. It is a room filled with brotherly love. And even though I am one of the lucky few with all of my limbs, I understand their feelings.

The nurses are most dedicated and devoted to their assignments. At times they can be demanding; and most of all they are caring and warm to the task when attending their patients. They are truly my angels! I learned to love and respect every one of them during my 10 months of treatment and rehab in three army general hospitals[*] where I finally received my honorable discharge from the Army Air Force.

---

[*] England General Hospital, Atlantic City, New Jersey

Bruns General Hospital, Santa Fe, New Mexico

Brooke General Hospital, Fort Sam Houston, San Antonio, Texas

IT'S THE SOLDIER!

When The Country Has Been In Need, It Has
Always Been The Soldier!
It's the soldier, not the newspaper which has given us
the freedom of the press-
It's the soldier, not the poet, who has given us freedom of speech-
It's the soldier, not the campus organizer, who has given
us the freedom to demonstrate-
It's the soldier, who salutes the flag, and serves under the flag-
It's the soldier whose coffin is draped with the flag,
who allows the protester to burn the flag-
And, it's the soldier who is called upon to defend our
way of life!   *Author unknown*

Presented By
National Sojourners

In case we find ourselves starting to believe all the anti-American Sentiment and negativity, we should remember England's Prime Minister Tony Blair's words during a recent interview. When asked by One of his Parliament members why he believes so much in America, he Said the following and I quote:

> "A simple way to take measure of a country is to look at how many Want in . . . And how many want out." Only two defining forces have Ever offered to die for you:
>
> 1.   Jesus Christ
> 2.   The American G. I.
>
> One died for your soul, the other for your freedom."

YOU MIGHT WANT TO PASS THIS On, AS MANY SEEM TO FORGET BOTH OF THEM.

SUPPLEMENT 2

Foggia, Italy Oct. 29, 1944

Foggia, Italy Oct.1944

HUNGARIAN
E REPÜLÖ EGY ELISMERVÉNYT AD ÖNNEK AZ ON ÁLTAL SZAMARA
NYUJTOTT SEGITSÉG MEGJUTALMAZÁSA CÉLJÁBÓL.
AZ ELISMERVÉNYT BEMUTATÁSA ALKALMÁVAL A SZÖVETSEGES
KATONAI HATÓSÁGOK BEVÁLTJÁK.
EZ JUTTATJA KIFEJEZÉSÜL A SZÖVETSÉGESEK, OSZINTE HALÁJA'T
A REPÜLÖJUK SZÁMÁRA ON ÁLTAL NYUJTOTT SEGITSÉGERT

POLISH
TEM LOTNIK WYPISZE TAKĄ POWINNOŚĆ O WYNAGRODZENIE PANU
DLA POMÓC KTURĄ PAN JÉMU UDZIELIT.
NA PRZEDSTAWIENIU OD TEGO SWIADECTWO PRZED WLADZYM
WOJSKOWYM ALIANSKYM, ZWROCIMY PANĄ KOSZTY.
RAZEM JEST TO WYRAZONE ZA DALSZĄ WOZIECZNOŚĆ ALIANSKĄ
ZA POMÓC DANEDLA NASZYCH LOTNIKÓW.

GERMAN
DER FLIEGER DEM SIE HILFE GELEISTET HABEN WIRD IHNEN EINEN
SCHEIN GEBEN WENN SIE DENSELBEN DEN ALLIIERTEN BEHÖRDEN
VORLEGEN, SO WERDEN SIE IHNEN IHRE UMKOSTEN ZURÜCKERSTATTEN
BEI DER WOLLEN WIR IHNEN UNSERN TIEILHERZIGSTEN DANK FÜR
DIE HILFE DIE SIE UNSEREN FLIEGERN GELEISTET HABEN, AUSSPRECHEN.

ITALIAN
QUESTO AVIATORE VI RILASCIERA UN CERTIFICATO PER COMPROVARE
L'AIUTO CHE GLI AVETE DATO, E LE AUTORITÀ MILITARI ALLEATE
VI RICOMPENSERANNO ADEGUATAMENTE PER QUESTO. ESSE VI
ESPRIMERANNO PURE LA GRATITUDINE DEGLI ALLEATI PER
L'ASSISTENZA DA VOI DATA AI NOSTRI AVIATORI

FRENCH
UN BILLET VOUS SERA DONNÉ PAR L'AVIATEUR AUQUEL VOUS AVEZ
PORTÉ AIDE.
SUR PRÉSENTATION DE CE BILLET AUX AUTORITÉS MILITAIRES
ALLIÉES VOUS SEREZ REMBOURSÉ DU MONTANT DES FRAIS QUE VOUS
AVEZ ENCOURUS.
EN MÊME TEMPS NOUS DESIRONS VOUS EXPRIMER L'EXTRÊME
RECONNAISSANCE POUR L'AIDE QUE VOUS AVEZ APPORTÉ A NOS
AVIATEURS.

U.S. ARMY AIR FORCE

IDENTIFICATION CARD
УДOCTOBEPEHИE ЛИЧHOCTИ
DOWÓD OSOBISTY
LEGITIMACE
LEGITIMACJA
SZEMELYAZONOSSAGI IGAZOLVÁNY
LEGITIMATION

I'M AN AMERICAN AIRMAN.
PLEASE TAKE ME TO YOUR COMMANDING OFFICER AND NOTIFY NEARES
AMERICAN OR BRITISH MILITARY MISSION IN BELGRADE, BUCHAREST,
POLTAVA OR OTHER NEARBY PLACE. ALSO, PLEASE ARRANGE FOR TRANS
PORTATION

THANK YOU

SHOW THIS TO RUSSIANS:

Я АМЕРИКАНСКИЙ ЛЕТЧИК
ПОЖАЛУЙСТА ПРЕДСТАВЬТЕ МЕНЯ ВАШЕМУ КОМАНДИРУ
И УВЕДОМИТЕ БЛИЖАЙШУЮ АМЕРИКАНСКУЮ ИЛИ
БРИТАНСКУЮ ВОЕННУЮ МИССИЮ В БЕЛГРАДЕ,
БУХАРЕСТЕ, ПОЛТАВЕ ИЛИ В ДРУГОМ БЛИЖАЙШ
МЕСТЕ. ТАКЖЕ РАСПОРЯДИТЕСЬ О ПЕРЕДВИЖЕНИИ.
БОЛЬШОЕ СПАСИВО !!

SELECTIVE SERVICE SYSTEM

January 30, 1943

TO: Achilles Kozakis
16 Flint Street
Lynn, Mass.

FROM: Chairman, Local Board No. 91, Lynn

SUBJECT: Induction.

1.   Please report to this office by telephone or
in person by Tuesday, February 9th, at 12 o'clock,
that you received induction notice to report at
the Houghton Branch Library, Breed Square, at
7:10 a.m., on Thursday morning, February 11th.
This is important.

2.   Please report at the Houghton Branch Library on
time.

Very respectfully yours,

Ralph W. Reeve, Chairman

Ly 2-8115

FOR VICTORY
BUY
UNITED
STATES
SAVINGS
BONDS
AND STAMPS

Local Board No. 91   **13**
Essex County   **009**

> JAN 30 1943 **091**
>
> 7 Central Square
> Lynn, Mass.
> (Stamp of Local Board.)

January 30, 1943
....
(Date of mailing)

ORDER TO REPORT FOR INDUCTION

The President of the United States,

To .... **Achilles** .... **Kozakis** ....
     (First name)   (Middle name)   (Last name)

Order No. .... **12061** ....

GREETING:

    Having submitted yourself to a Local Board composed of your neighbors for the purpose of determining your availability for training and service in the armed forces of the United States, you are hereby

notified that you have now been selected for training and service in the .... **Army and Navy** ....
               (Army, Navy, Marine Corps)

    You will, therefore, report to the Local Board named above at .... **Houghton Branch Library, Breed S**
               (Place of reporting)

at ....**7:10 a.** m., on the .... **11th** .... day of .... **February** ...., 19 **43**.
  (Hour of reporting)

    This Local Board will furnish transportation to an induction station of the service for which you have been selected. You will there be examined and if accepted for training and service, you will then be inducted into the stated branch of the service.

    Persons reporting to the induction station in some instances may be rejected for physical or other reasons. It is well to keep this in mind in arranging your affairs, to prevent any undue hardship if you are rejected at the induction station. If you are employed, you should advise your employer of this notice and of the possibility that you may not be accepted at the induction station. Your employer can then be prepared to replace you if you are accepted, or to continue your employment if you are rejected.

    ~~If you are not accepted, you will be furnished transportation to the place where you were living when ordered to report for induction by this Local Board.~~

    Willful failure to report promptly to this Local Board at the hour and on the day named in this notice is a violation of the Selective Training and Service Act of 1940 and subjects the violator to fine and imprisonment. Bring with you sufficient clothing for 3 days.

    You must keep this form and bring it with you when you report to the Local Board.

    If you are so far removed from your own Local Board that reporting in compliance with this Order will be a serious hardship and you desire to report to a Local Board in the area of which you are now located, go immediately to that Local Board and make written request for transfer of your delivery for induction, taking this Order with you.

....
Member of Local Board.

~~D. S. S. Form 150~~
~~(Revised 4/9/41)~~
D.S.S. Form 150

Ralph W. Reeve, Chairman

Honorable Discharge

This is to certify that

ACHILLES KOZAKIS 31 430 427 Staff Sergeant

726th Bomb Squadron 451st Bomb Group

Army of the United States

is hereby Honorably Discharged from the military service of the United States of America.

This certificate is awarded as a testimonial of Honest and Faithful Service to this country.

Given at BROOKE GENERAL HOSPITAL
          Fort Sam Houston, Texas

Date   29 May 1946

E M SMITH
COL MEDICAL CORPS

ENLISTED RECORD AND REPORT OF SEPARATION
HONORABLE DISCHARGE

1. LAST NAME - FIRST NAME - MIDDLE INITIAL	2. ARMY SERIAL NO.	3. GRADE	4. ARM OR SERVICE	5. COMPONENT
Kozakis Achilles	31 430 427	S/Sgt	AAF	AUS

6. ORGANIZATION	7. DATE OF SEPARATION	8. PLACE OF SEPARATION
726th Bomb Sq 451st Bomb Gp	29 May 46	Brooke Gen Hosp FSHTex

9. PERMANENT ADDRESS FOR MAILING PURPOSES	10. DATE OF BIRTH	11. PLACE OF BIRTH
16 Flint Street Lynn (Essex) Massachusetts	19 Oct 23	Lynn Massachusetts

12. ADDRESS FROM WHICH EMPLOYMENT WILL BE SOUGHT	13. COLOR EYES	14. COLOR HAIR	15. HEIGHT	16. WEIGHT	17. NO. DEPEND.
See 9	Brown	Brown	5' 9"	154 lbs.	0

18. RACE	19. MARITAL STATUS	20. U.S. CITIZEN	27. CIVILIAN OCCUPATION AND NO.
WHITE X	SINGLE X	YES X	Draftsman Mechanical 0-43,180

MILITARY HISTORY

22. DATE OF INDUCTION	23. DATE OF ENLISTMENT	24. DATE OF ENTRY INTO ACTIVE SERVICE	25. PLACE OF ENTRY INTO SERVICE
17 Jan 44		17 Jan 44	Boston Massachusetts

26. SELECTIVE SERVICE DATA YES X NO	27. LOCAL S.S. BOARD NO.	28. COUNTY AND STATE	29. HOME ADDRESS AT TIME OF ENTRY INTO SERVICE
	91	Essex Massachusetts	16 Flint Street Lynn (Essex) Mass

30. MILITARY OCCUPATIONAL SPECIALTY AND NO.		31. MILITARY QUALIFICATION AND DATE
Airplane Armored Gunner	612	Aviation Badge Gunner AAF Reg 35-30 11 Dec 43 Air Crew Member Badge AAF Reg 35-30 1944

32. BATTLES AND CAMPAIGNS

Northern France GO 33 WD 45 Rhineland GO 40 WD 45
North Apennines GO 40 WD 45 Po Valley GO 40 WD 45 Central Europe GO 40 WD 45

33. DECORATIONS AND CITATIONS
World War II Victory Medal Purple Heart GO not available 19 Feb 45
Good Conduct Medal GO not available Air Medal GO 4714 Hq 15th AF 27 Nov 44
European African Middle Eastern Service Medal American Theater Service Medal

34. WOUNDS RECEIVED IN ACTION
5 Feb 45 European Theater

35. LATEST IMMUNIZATION DATES				36. SERVICE OUTSIDE CONTINENTAL U. S. AND RETURN		
SMALLPOX	TYPHOID	TETANUS	OTHER (specify) Typhus	DATE OF DEPARTURE	DESTINATION	DATE OF ARRIVAL
1 Feb 45	1 Feb 45	6 Apr 44	1 Feb 45	4 Oct 44	EAME Theater	20 Oct 44

37. TOTAL LENGTH OF SERVICE						38. HIGHEST GRADE HELD			
CONTINENTAL SERVICE			FOREIGN SERVICE						
YEARS	MONTHS	DAYS	YEARS	MONTHS	DAYS	S/Sgt	25 May 45	US	12 Jun 45
1	8	4	0	8	9				

39. PRIOR SERVICE

None

FOR CONVENIENCE, A CERTIFICATE OF DISCHARGE no 200-90 ...

40. REASON AND AUTHORITY FOR SEPARATION Certificate of Disability for Discharge Section 1 AR-615-361
4 Nov 44 and 1st Indorsement Brooke General Hospital Fort Sam Houston, Texas 27 May 46

41. SERVICE SCHOOLS ATTENDED	42. EDUCATION (Years)
Specialized Crs in Emerson Turret Aerial Gunnery School Laredo Texas	Grammar 8 High School 4 College 0

PAY DATA

43. LONGEVITY FOR PAY PURPOSES			44. MUSTERING OUT PAY		45. SOLDIER DEPOSITS	46. TRAVEL PAY	47. TOTAL AMOUNT, NAME OF DISBURSING OFFICER
YEARS	MONTHS	DAYS	TOTAL	THIS PAYMENT	None		
2	4	13	300	100		106.30	269.81 A O WALSH COL FD

INSURANCE NOTICE

IMPORTANT If premium is not paid when due or within thirty-one days thereafter, insurance will lapse. Make checks or money orders payable to the TREASURER OF THE U. S., AND FORWARD TO COLLECTIONS SUBDIVISION, VETERANS ADMINISTRATION, WASHINGTON 25, D. C.

48. KIND OF INSURANCE	49. HOW PAID	50. Effective Date of Allot. ment Discontinuance	51. Date of Next Premium Due (One month after 50)	52. PREMIUM DUE EACH MONTH	53. INTENTION OF VETERAN TO
Nat. Serv. X U.S. Govt.	Allotment X Direct to V.A.	WAIVER IN EFFECT		6.50	Continue X Discontinue

54. REMARKS (This space for completion of above items or entry of other items specified in W. D. Directives)
Lapel button issued ASR score (2 Sept 45) 73
** 1st Oak Leaf Cluster to Air Medal GO 4 Hq 15th AF 2 Jan 45
** 2nd Oak Leaf Cluster to Air Medal GO 12 Hq Hq 15th AF 19 Feb 45
** 3rd Oak Leaf Cluster to Air Medal GO not available 27 Apr 45

56. SIGNATURE OF PERSON BEING SEPARATED	57. PERSONNEL OFFICER (Type name, grade and organization - signature)
Achilles Kozakis	JOHN F GEDERS Capt MAC

WD AGO Form 53-55 This form supersedes all previous editions of this form.

SEPARATION QUALIFICATION RECORD
SAVE THIS FORM. IT WILL NOT BE REPLACED IF LOST

This record of job assignments and special training received in the Army is furnished to the soldier when he leaves the service. In its preparation, information is taken from available Army records and supplemented by personal interview. The information about civilian education and work experience is based on the individual's own statements. The veteran may present this document to former employers, prospective employers, representatives of schools or colleges, or use it in any other way that may prove beneficial to him.

1. LAST NAME—FIRST NAME—MIDDLE INITIAL			MILITARY OCCUPATIONAL ASSIGNMENTS		
KOZAKIS ACHILLES			10. MONTHS	11. GRADE	12. MILITARY OCCUPATIONAL SPECIALTY
2. ARMY SERIAL NO.	3. GRADE	4. SOCIAL SECURITY NO.	2	Pvt	Basic Training, AAF (521)
31 450 427	S/Sgt	000-00-0000	10	S/Sgt	Airplane Armored
5. PERMANENT MAILING ADDRESS (Street, City, County, State)					Gunner (612)
18 Flint Street					
Lynn (Essex) Massachusetts					
6. DATE OF ENTRY INTO ACTIVE SERVICE	7. DATE OF SEPARATION	8. DATE OF BIRTH			
17 Jan 1944	29 May 1946	19 Oct 1923			
9. PLACE OF SEPARATION					
BROOKE GENERAL HOSPITAL					
FORT SAM HOUSTON, TEXAS					

SUMMARY OF MILITARY OCCUPATIONS

13. TITLE—DESCRIPTION—RELATED CIVILIAN OCCUPATION

AIRPLANE ARMORED GUNNER: Served with 451st Bomb Group, 726th Bomb Squadron in the European Theater of Operations. Inspected, repaired and maintained all aircraft armament, including bomb release mechanism, airplane cannon, machine guns and auxiliary equipment, made daily inspections of guns, disassembled them and replaced worn out parts, cleaned and lubricated the guns and turrets.

MILITARY EDUCATION

NAME OR TYPE OF SCHOOL—COURSE OR CURRICULUM—DURATION—DESCRIPTION

Attended the Gunnery School at Laredo, Texas; completed a 2-month course in maintenance of guns and turrets.

CIVILIAN EDUCATION

HIGHEST GRADE COMPLETED	16. DEGREES OR DIPLOMAS	17. YEAR LEFT SCHOOL	OTHER TRAINING OR SCHOOLING	
	High School		18. COURSE—NAME AND ADDRESS OF SCHOOL—DATE	19. DURATION
12	Diploma	1943		
18. NAME AND ADDRESS OF LAST SCHOOL ATTENDED			None	
Lynn Classical High School				
Lynn, Massachusetts				
MAJOR COURSE OF STUDY				
Vocational				

CIVILIAN OCCUPATIONS

22. TITLE—NAME AND ADDRESS OF EMPLOYER—INCLUSIVE DATES—DESCRIPTION

DRAFTSMAN, MECHANICAL: Was employed by General Electric Company for seven months at Lynn, Massachusetts, to 1944; specialized in making rough drafting sketches of proposed mechanical devices, and then drawing necessary scale drawings of parts of machines from specifications; made detail and assembly drawings of jigs, fixtures, tools, and mechanical parts.

ADDITIONAL INFORMATION

REMARKS

None

SIGNATURE OF PERSON BEING SEPARATED	SIGNATURE OF SEPARATION CLASSIFICATION	NAME OF OFFICER (Type or Stamped)
		KENNETH H. ANDERSON
		2d Lt AGD

Karakis Achilleos ASN 31430427 GR S/SGT

Date **17 JUL 1945** AAFRS. No. 1, Atlantic City, N. J.

I CERTIFY THAT THE ABOVE NAMED INDIVIDUAL IS ENTITLED TO WEAR THE FOLLOWING AWARDS, DECORATIONS, CITATIONS, & THEATER RIBBONS MARKED "AUTHORIZED"

GOOD CONDUCT Authorized	
AIR MEDAL Authorized	(*2*)+*1* OLC TO AIR MEDAL
DFC Authorized	( ) OLC TO DFC
PURPLE HEART Authorized	(*1*) OLC TO PURPLE HEART
AMERICAN THEATER Authorized	AMERICAN DEFENSE

ASIATIC-PACIFIC THEATER WITH ( ) BRONZE STARS	
EAME THEATER Authorized	WITH (*5*) BRONZE STARS
DISTINGUISHED UNIT BADGE Authorized	(*2*) OLC TO UNIT BADGE
AVIATION BADGE: AIR CREW MEMBER ( ) AERIAL GUNNER (✓) PILOT ( ) BOMBARDIER ( ) NAVIGATOR ( ) ( ) Authorized	
OVERSEAS SERVICE BARS (*1*) Authorized	
OTHER AWARDS:	

AAFRS NO. 1, FORM 153
(REVISED 17/JAN/45)

ACHILLES KOZAKIS

To you who answered the call of your country and served in its Armed Forces to bring about the total defeat of the enemy, I extend the heartfelt thanks of a grateful Nation. As one of the Nation's finest, you undertook the most severe task one can be called upon to perform. Because you demonstrated the fortitude, resourcefulness and calm judgment necessary to carry out that task, we now look to you for leadership and example in further exalting our country in peace.

Harry Truman

THE WHITE HOUSE

ARMY AIR FORCES
Certificate of Appreciation
FOR WAR SERVICE

TO

Achilles Kozakis

I CANNOT meet you personally to thank you for a job well done; nor can I hope to put in written words the great hope I have for your success in future life.

Together we built the striking force that swept the Luftwaffe from the skies and broke the German power to resist. The total might of that striking force was then unleashed upon the Japanese. Although you no longer play an active military part, the contribution you made to the Air Forces was essential in making us the greatest team in the world.

The ties that bound us under stress of combat must not be broken in peacetime. Together we share the responsibility for guarding our country in the air. We who stay will never forget the part you have played while in uniform. We know you will continue to play a comparable role as a civilian. As our ways part, let me wish you God speed and the best of luck on your road in life. Our gratitude and respect go with you.

COMMANDING GENERAL
ARMY AIR FORCES

30 July 1951

Mr. Achilles Kozakis
16 Flint Street
Lynn, Massachusetts

Dear   Mr. Kozakis:

The Air Force takes pride in forwarding you a Certificate of
Valor conferred upon you by the Commanding General of the Air Forces
in the Mediterranean Theater of Operations in recognition of your
achievements in that theater during World War II.

This certificate does not constitute a basis for the award of
any decoration, but is proffered as tangible evidence of your significant contribution to the Air Forces in the Mediterranean Theater.

Sincerely,

JOHN McM. GULICK
Lt Colonel, USAF
Office, Director of Military Personnel

1 Incl
   Certificate

B 4 8 1 2 6

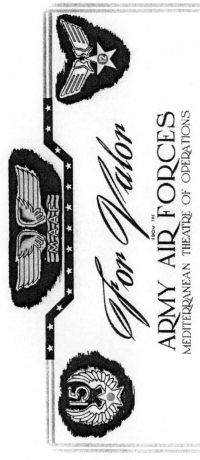

For Valor

FROM THE

ARMY AIR FORCES
MEDITERRANEAN THEATRE OF OPERATIONS

It is with great personal pride that I present this certificate to S/Sgt. Achilles Kozakis 31430427 Gunner who, having been engaged in 35 combat missions in the Mediterranean theatre in air-battles of great intensity, has gallantly and repeatedly carried the offensive against heavy opposition to the heart of the enemy and has, by his unfaltering courage, earned the gratitude and praise of his fellow — countrymen, as well as his Commander.

Lieutenant General U.S. Army
Commanding

ORDERS)
)   E X T R A C T   6 July 1944
NUMBER 52)

   5. Under auth contained in AR 35-1480 the fol named EM are placed on
dy involving participation in reg and frequent aerial flights until reld by
competent auth, eff this date:

TECHNICAL SERGEANTS		CORPORALS CONT'D	
Bassett, Robert M.	31038114	Beltzer, Harold	12121701
Delaney, John P.	6289405	Betterolli, Anthony J.	32951468
Cheshewalla, Joseph E.	18054071	Bierut, Edward J.	12169442
		Blaise, Ernest I.	31378553
STAFF SERGEANTS		Bloedel, Hugo D.	36655851
		Breuer, Frederick A.	32937345
Bailey, Chester E.	11013084	Brogan, Harold J.	35649141
Campbell, Charles F.	18062860	Bubonko, James P.	33761548
Cassiano, Wallace N.	11027139	Bueker, Donald A.	36110295
Frankel, Stanley	12022533	Bumpus, Walter B.	14077763
Fuller, Theodore F.	16033085	Cabe, Frederick W.	12147123
Paine, Alfred D.	11027842	Carey, Edgar R.	32951708
Sloan, George A.	34096014	Carpenter, Charles J.	32952465
		Carreon, Antonio	39289348
SERGEANTS		Carrington, Walter A.	11101309
		Cassandra, Ralph M.	42045844
Greer, James H.	14043525	Ciccotti, Victor	42003658
Nordwall, Donald E.	20620961	Cirinna, Emmanuele S.	11093129
Bean, Elton	36561046	Cohen, Seymour L.	32926763
Edelblute, Jack L.	35422794	Collins, John	32910583
Freedman, William J.	31108710	Connell, James J.	32914071
Friedlander, Alfred R.	12143064	Cook, Marion E.	14200910
Mangels, John H.	32655692	Corradini, Ferdinand P.	31447395
Monk, George F.	33005127	Cramer, Ralph J.	32908793
Montgomery, John B.	17053385	Crothers, Joseph	36536619
Probst, Robert T.	12034513	Dari, Leponty A.	20200540
Sinclair, Tobe W.	38473660	Declercq, Gaston A.	32890734
Smock, Harold L.	18086525	De Marco, Frank A.	32864125
Stanton, Charles W.	12165445	De Simone, Alessio	31298105
Twiest, John H. Jr.	11070549	Diamond, Harold H.	32460733
Young, Millard B.	11035937	Draus, Henry D.	31331270
		Eaton, Reuben B. Jr.	31448201
CORPORALS		Edwards, David W.	35607301
		Eggert, Roland W.	32951658
Gallagher, Jesse M.	13030396	Ellefson, John N.	16082474
West, Robert W.	6932711	Everett, Luther M. Jr.	38423907
Apsel, Morris I.	32821494	Falin, Earl L.	33532000
Balzer, Lauren A.	19201417	Fedora, John	33055567
Bassett, Roger F.	31346121	Fisher, Henry	32778793
Bastarache, Joseph N.	11131031	Flammer, Robert G.	33616891
Beattie, Robert J. Jr.	39203811	Flynn, Charles M.	12139061

CORPORALS CONT'D

Frenette, John D.	31211500
Fritton, Edward G.	12169666
Gadol, Morris S.	32709492
Galbreath, Harold E.	37384453
Geland, William E.	11104108
George, Harold E.	17168710
Gertig, Albert C.	31363751
Giglio, Vincent, Jr.	34788102
Goodner, Howard G.	34726638
Gordon, Robert D.	36465130
Grab, William G.	32807558
Grabuski, Leonard P.	33505524
Gregorian, Harry	16151300
Halverson, Lester K.	6892894
Hardick, Peter, Jr.	13098304
Harper, James F.	34651469
Harris, Douglas M.	35361656
Hart, Curtis E.	42047463
Hart, Julius A. Jr.	14155998
Hayes, Albert C.	11103955
Hedrick, Wilmer R.	33827290
Held, Robert L. Jr.	33006812
Herrell, William O.	37721590
Hicks, Thomas W.	32782971
Hildebrand, Clyde, Jr.	35760355
Hoffman, Donald L.	33763289
Hoysen, Robert L.	37669219
Hough, Thomas E.	35731849
Householder, William A.	17116380
Iadeolisi, Alfred J.	31363495
Jackson, Raymond H.	31372963
Jangers, Eugene D.	37656676
Kadzewski, Walter W.	32951979
Karr, Martin	32707067
Keeler, John L.	11116109
Kalonek, Michael	13106628
Panazzolo, Vito S.	12083580
Parkinson, Michael V.	36806882
Parrish, James M.	14174329
Perelman, Jack L.	15121704
Pettinari, Dominic	19085263
Player, Harry A. Jr.	12125611
Popplewell, Robert H.	37520860
Realley, George W. Jr.	33600362
Rockwell, Francis X.	13054012
Rodriguez, Joseph N.	16083229
Rosen, Jerome L.	12110985
Rowe, Austin L.	33610265
Sarton, Edward J.	31300454
Sarver, Richard C.	13107884
Schetter, Joseph L.	35229182

Schnoebelen, Clement R.	15342176
Schwartz, Leonard	14192402
Sivori, Stanley B.	35696185
Snyder, John M.	13068431
Solorzano, José J.	18138085
Street, James T.	12138650
Tegland, George I.	39210038
Trainor, Thomas J. Jr.	32810230
Trimble, Raymond L.	35787495
Turner, James H.	14192589
Vogel, Wallace G.	12159718
Winslow, Roy N.	16159673
Wishba, Joseph J.	36670853
Wolf, Jack W.	37478273
Yaffe, Earl D.	16169433
Young, Fred P.	35658423
Young, Robert P.	36595361
Zafferano, Paul J.	32793462
Kerbel, Stephen P.	32926374
Kile, Thomas E.	36851962
Kiteley, Leonard W.	36637740
Knight, Jack M.	35757088
Kovacs, Michael R. Jr.	32757276
Kraemer, John H.	16115366
Kreher, Elmer R. Jr.	32732772
Kutschera, Robert	11104152
Latzka, Kenneth H.	37550080
Lee, Clifford F.	32952457
Lehman, George E.	12093961
Longacre, James E.	32952679
Love, John P.	14180802
Lueders, John J.	34883541
Lyon, Ludwig G.	31144797
McCarthy, John J.	42062824
McCue, Thomas E.	39124905
McGowan, Alan C.	31398640
McLean, Frank D.	33587374
McNeely, David E.	34609931
Maddox, John B.	34645619
Mantini, Joseph P.	31255253
Marlow, James M.	12066350
Martenucci, Frank	36860162
Martin, Donald S.	16159517
Martin, Warren L.	36877640
Morehouse, Roland L.	3646073C
Morris, Daniel B.	34677480
Murphy, James H.	42001089
Neal, Robert	16151632
Nelson, Erik A.	38477968
Nietz, Gilford P.	36680798
O'Connell, Matthew E.	32889097

Order No. 52, Par 5, Hq's Sec. "E", dd 6 July 1944 cont'd.

PRIVATES FIRST CLASS

Bailey, Ernest E.	37707169	Irion, Gerald A.	36893777
Bilanych, George	35927231	Jabro, John P.	36869610
Bliss, David M.	31416622	Jacobs, Edward B.	36830766
Bobrowiecki, Henry J.	31421816	Jacobs, Herbert B.	16177226
Bogseth, Clifford R.	12221338	Kalman, Lawrence J.	42064782
Brennan, John C.	12206828	Kammer, Jack K.	13110855
Brewster, Raymond E.	20242528	Kane, Earnest J.	33657890
Bricker, Leo	12227538	Keesling, William F.	35901848
Britson, Reugen W.	37684853	Kelly, John D.	33808339
Broitzman, Curtis L.	36840189	Kelpzig, Robert B.	12130326
Churacas, Christy V.	12226105	Klinedinst, Charles F.	33871971
Collins, Edgar S.	35848495	Knight, Alton E.	31428340
Coombs, Hudson W.	34923004	Kniskern, Howard J.	12100989
Corradetti, Anthony A.	33793945	Koffler, Irwin	42050296
Cervacchioli, Louis R.	33809278	Koly, Stanley P.	35230981
Courter, Paul E.	12238691	Koury, Michael F.	35933124
Crabbe, Bruce G.	12080738	Kozakis, Achilles	31430427
Crabtree, Norman J.	35298485	Loman, Richard J.	12239763
Craft, Norris C.	35770346	Lonergan, Donald F.	12176341
DeConto, Oscar L.	31356182	Lowry, Boyd N.	38342406
Dickelman, Merle W.	16145131	Lusk, Ora C.	34917421
DiGregorio, Rosario P.	32970901	Oddo, Paul B.	42053476
D'Hogge, Marcel E.	16078079	Olivier, Joseph D. Jr.	31384852
Eastman, John M. Jr.	11086290	Olson, Lloyd N.	39922155
Foster, Harry S.	36046715	Onischuk, Alek	31409559
Gaylord, Edward C.	42103320	Parsons, George F.	31409154
Givans, Clifford P.	35812779	Patton, Robert E.	38512695
Green, Herbert E.	31370415	Pearson, Irving J.	31430355
Grieshop, Jerome B.	35629588	Perkins, John W.	14117130
Griffiths, Elmer, Jr.	35299784	Peterson, Lawrence A.	36777730
Gutleber, George S.	42102869	Peterson, Robert E.	16054935
Gysan, William H. Jr.	11140789	Petlock, Arthur H.	31417311
Hagans, Jack L.	35902572	Piccolo, Vincent	31359541
Hall, E. C.	34917444	Plasse, Edward J.	31431344
Hardy, Charles E.	15128001	Prescott, Fitzhugh	36872608
Hargan, Donald J.	37632368	Price, Eugene W.	39923260
Harrigan, Joseph J.	31362398	Pultz, Edward H.	12228618
Heineler, Bernard R.	12217606	Regennitter, Robert W.	37679105
Holmes, Thomas H. Jr.	32947203	Reinhardt, John L.	14167047
Hoskinson, Robert N.	35812637	Roberts, Roland L.	31348957
Hudson, Alva T.	35883139	Robertson, Virgil A.	39721017
Hughes, Ernest	35883140	Rodriguez, Demetrio P. Jr.	39862762
Hull, Elliott J. Jr.	38497153	Russell, Charles H.	42069392
Irwin, John R.	35229733	Rzencki, Henry R.	13090656
Jahier, Louis J.	12191723	Sabulis, John A.	11138714
Janison, Luther N.	35698721	Schapiro, Sherman B.	39417114
Johnson, Charles P.	36837336	Searan, Gordon W.	12089812
Justis, Edwin F.	33645998	Seanons, Olecn	39922829
Heiderman, Joseph E.	12238722	Sepne, George	33679450
Hoffmann, Vernon E.	37413948	Soraydarian, Albert	42064928
Horowitz, Herbert B.	12144099	Sheehan, George J.	11085595

-3-

PRIVATES FIRST CLASS CONT'D

Silverman, Edward L.	12228301
Skyles, Donald J.	39921824
Smith, John E.	12217144
Smith, Richard H.	31332762
Sornaruga, Joseph A.	31381448
Stavrogalos, Nick M.	15108720
Sternberg, Roger W.	19201908
Struppa, Charles E.	16080788
Sutton, Charles A.	17105931
Swain, Vernon R. R.	19144277
Swenson, Gordon J.	17111084
Taylor, Alfred L.	31362193
Tessier, John D.	11086215
Thome, Benjamin J. Jr.	42092944
Thornton, William F.	42103960
Towns, Norman F.	11123104
Trahan, Claude J.	11086206
Tranter, Robert L.	12174866
Tuttle, Ernest A.	31261873
Valent, Vincent V. Jr.	33715904
Vance, James E.	35442619
Vance, Roland C. L.	38564213
Vannucci, Osvaldo J.	39419641
Vazna, George H.	31448058
Vickers, Frank S.	11128297
Vigor, Alfred J.	11104831
Vollrath, William L.	36696762
Wages, Earl R.	34848594
Walinski, Walter	32939214
Wallace, Grier S.	14203297

PRIVATES FIRST CLASS CONT'D

Warner, Marvin R.	36896527
Wasek, Marion	42103480
Wehrhan, Maurice H.	17169628
Weiler, Kenneth J.	37676939
Weisser, Benjamin	12120349
Welch, Ralph T.	36485910
Wells, Raymond R.	32859487
Wheble, Herbert J.	11108467
Wiggins, Lyle D.	31398395
Wilkins, Jack R.	33641906
Zabit, Thomas W. Jr.	31410474
Zappavigna, Joseph F.	32987793
Zitron, Carl	35919439

PRIVATES

Beal, Charles E.	15125374
Drake, Charles W.	13111331
Farling, Howard J.	13123401
Paffenbach, Earl W.	15108563
Perry, Harold E.	14071652
Poernich, Ivan G.	17114551
Sunde, Donald K.	17065866
Sweeney, James T.	12200874
Tessitore, Louis M.	31292762
Valentine, William A. Jr.	13157129
Woolf, Alan P.	12176241

By order of Major HODGES:

OFFICIAL:

[signature]

JOHN F. RASH,
Captain, Air Corps,
Adjutant.

JOHN F. RASH,
Captain, Air Corps,
Adjutant.

27 November 1944
(Date)

GENERAL ORDERS)
:
NUMBER   4714)   E X T R A C T

Award of the Air Medal . . . . Section . . . I

SECTION I - AWARD OF THE AIR MEDAL

Under the provisions of AR 600-45, as amended, and pursuant to authority contained in Circular No. 69, Headquarters NATOUSA, 10 July 1944, the Air Medal, in the categories as listed, is awarded the following named personnel, **726** Bombardment Squadron, Air Corps, United States Army, residence as indicated, for meritorious achievement in aerial flight while participating in sustained operational activities against the enemy between the dates as indicated, and/or, for meritorious achievement in aerial flight while performing an act of merit as indicated:

AIR MEDAL

    *   *   *   *
ACHILLES KOZAKIS, 31430427, Corporal, Lynn, Massachusets. 5 to 17 November 1944.
    *   *   *   *

By command of Major General TWINING:

                                        R. K. TAYLOR,
                                        Colonel, GSC,
                                        Chief of Staff.
OFFICIAL:

    /s/ J. M. Ivins
    J. M. IVINS,   A TRUE EXTRACT COPY:
    Colonel, AGD,
    Adjutant General.   C. E. Campbell Jr.
                             C. E. CAMPBELL,
                             CWO, USA.

HEADQUARTERS
FIFTEENTH AIR FORCE
APO 520

C-UPD-hch

GENERAL ORDERS)
                  :   E X T R A C T   2 January 1945
NUMBER   4   )

Section
Awards of the Air Medal and/or Oak Leaf Cluster for the Air Medal..........I

SECTION I --AWARDS OF AIR MEDAL AND/OR OAK LEAF CLUSTER FOR THE AIR MEDAL

Under the provisions of AR600-45, as amended, and pursuant to authority
contained in Circular No. 89, MATOUSA, 10 July 1944, the Air Medal and/or
Oak Leaf Cluster for the Air Medal, in the categories as listed, is awarded
the following named personnel, Air Corps, Army of the United States, residence as indicated for meritorious achievement in aerial flight while participating in sustained operational activities against the enemy between
the dates as indicated:

*   *   *   *   *

FIRST OAK LEAF CLUSTER (BRONZE)
ACHILLES MORARIS, 31430427, Sergeant, Lynn, Massachusetts.
18 November to 27 December 1944.

*   *   *   *   *

By command of Major General TWINING:

R.K. TAYLOR,
Colonel, GSC,
Chief of Staff.

OFFICIAL:

/s/ J.M. Ivins,
J.M. IVINS,
Adjutant General

A TRUE EXTRACT COPY:

ALBERT F. OGO
Captain, Air Corps,
Adjutant.

R E S T R I C T E D

HEADQUARTERS
451ST BOMBARDMENT GROUP (H)
APO #520   US ARMY

19 February 1945.

GENERAL ORDERS)
              :
Number   12)

    Under the provisions of AR 600-45, as amended, and pursuant to authority contained in letter Headquarters, 15th Air Force, Subject: "Award of the Purple Heart", dtd 1 February 1944, the Purple Heart is awarded to the following named personnel, Air Corps, United States Army, for wounds received while participating in aerial flight against the armed enemy. Place of injury, date and residence as indicated:

    *   *   *   *

ACHILLES (NMI) KOZAKIS, 31430427, Staff Sergeant, Austria, 7 February 1945, Lynn, Massachusetts,.

CASIMER J. CZACHOROWSKI, 35058374, Private, Austria, 7 February 1945, Cleveland, Ohio.

    *   *   *   *

    By order of Colonel STEFONOWICZ:

OFFICIAL:

/s/ LYNN J. BARTLETT, JR.,
/t/ LYNN J. BARTLETT, JR.,
Major, Air Corps,
Adjutant.

LYNN J. BARTLETT, JR.,
Major, Air Corps,
Adjutant.

A TRUE EXTRACT COPY:

ALBERT F. OG.,
Captain, Air Corps,
Adjutant.

COMBAT RECORD OF: ACHILLES (NMI) KOZAKIS

31430427

(NAME)

DATE (MISSION)	MISSION NUMBER	PLACE OF COMBAT (COUNTRY)	HOURS
11-5-44	1	Yugoslavia	4:00
11-6-44	2	Austria	7:30
11-16-44	3	Germany	7:30
11-17-44	4	Germany	5:00
11-18-44	5	Italy	6:00
11-19-44	6	Austria	7:00
11-20-44	7	Germany	5:30
12-6-44	8	Yugoslavia	6:45
12-15-44	9	Austria	7:40
12-20-44	10	Austria	7:15
12-25-44	11	Austria	8:00
12-26-44	12	Poland	8:30
12-27-44	13	Italy	5:30
1-5-44	14	Yugoslavia	5:45
1-20-45	15	Austria	7:00
2-1-45	16	Austria	8:00
2-7-45	17	Austria	7:45
2-14-45	18	Austria	7:45
2-20-45	19	Italy	6:15
2-22-45	20	Germany	5:15
2-28-45	21	Italy	7:30
3-2-45	22	Austria	8:00
3-4-45	23	Austria	7:30
3-21-45	24	Austria	6:30
3-26-45	25	Austria	8:30
4-2-45	26	Austria	7:00
4-5-45	27	Italy	5:45
4-9-45	28	Italy	5:00
4-10-45	29	Italy	4:45
4-19-45	30	Italy	7:00
4-20-45	31	Italy	6:30
4-21-45	32	Italy	7:00
4-23-45	33	Italy	6:15
4-24-45	34	Italy	7:00
4-26-45	35	Italy	7:45
	35		245:45

Charles W. Atterholt

CHARLES W. ATTERHOLT, Capt. AC
Operations Officer (RANK OF
RESPONSIBLE OFFICER)

NAME ___ACHILLES (N.I) KOZARIS___ ASN ___31430427___

RANK Cpl. POSITION GG ORGANIZATION ___764th_ Sq.

DATE	TARGET	MISSION	HOURS	SORTIES	TOTAL HOURS	FOR EARLY RETURNS PUT CAUSE IN THIS COLUMN
11-5-44	Sarajevo, Yugo.	1	4:00	1	4:00	
11-6-44	Vienna, Austria	2	7:30		11:30	
11-16-44	Munich, Germany	3	7:30		19:00	
11-17-44	Blechhammer, Ger.	4	8:00		27:00	
11-18-44	Verona, Italy	5	6:00		33:00	
11-19-44	Vienna, Austria	6	7:00		40:00	
11-20-44	Blechhammer, Ger.	7	8:30		48:30	
12-6-44	Graz, Yugoslavia	8	6:45		55:15	
12-15-44	Linz, Austria	9	7:40		62:55	
12-20-44	Linz, Austria	10	7:15		70:10	
12-25-44	Wells, Austria	11	8:00		78:10	
12-26-44	Osweicim, Poland	12	8:30		86:40	
12-27-44	Venzone Viaduct	13	5:30		92:10	
1-5-44	Zagreb, Yugoslavia	14	5:45		97:55	
1-30-45	Linz, Austria	15	7:00		104:45	
2-1-45	Vienna, Austria	16	8:00		112:45	
2-7-45	Vienna, Austria	17	7:45		120:30	
2-14-45	Moosbierbaum, Aus	18	7:45		128:15	
2-20-45	Pola, Italy	19	6:15		134:30	
2-22-45	Rosenheim, Germany	20	8:15		142:45	
2-28-45	Bolzano, Italy	21	7:30		150:15	
3-2-45	Linz, Austria	22	8:00		158:15	
3-4-45	Graz, Yugoslavia	23	7:30		165:45	
3-22-45	Bruck, Austria	24	6:30		172:15	
3-23-45	Straszhof, Austria	25	8:30		180:45	
4-3-45	St. Polten, Austria	26	7:00		187:45	
4-5-45	Brescia, Italy	27	5:45		193:30	
4-9-45	Northern Italy	28	5:00		198:50	
4-17-45	Northern Italy	29	4:45		204:15	
4-19-45	Avisio, Italy	30	7:00		211:15	
4-20-45	Lusia RdBridge, Italy	31	6:30		217:45	
4-21-45	Attnang-Puchheim, Italy	32	7:00		224:45	
4-23-45	Jadia Road Bridge, It.	33	6:15		231:00	
4-24-45	Severeto R/K, Italy	34	7:00		238:00	
4-25-45	Linz, Austria	35	7:30	2	245:30	

INDIVIDUAL FLIGHT RECORD

(1) SERIAL NO. 31430427 (2) NAME Fozakis   Achilles   nmi (3) RANK Cpl (4) AGE
                              LAST   MIDDLE
(5) PERS. CLASS   (6) BRANCH Air Corps   (7) STATION APO 520
(8) ORGANIZATION ASSIGNED   15th   45th   451st   726th   ATTACHED FOR FLYING
                         AIR FORCE   COMMAND   WING   GROUP   SQUADRON   DETACHMENT
(9) ORGANIZATION ATTACHED
                         AIR FORCE   COMMAND   WING   GROUP   SQUADRON   DETACHMENT
(10) PRESENT RATING & DATE   (11) ORIGINAL RATING & DATE
(12) TRANSFERRED FROM   POE   (13) FLIGHT RESTRICTIONS
(15) TRANSFERRED TO   APO 520   (14) TRANSFER DATE   10-1-44

(16) PERS CLASS	RANK	RTG.	A. F.	COMMAND	WING	GROUP NO.	TYPE	SQUADRON NO.	TYPE	STATION	MO. YR.	(17) MONTH October 19 44

DAY	AIRCRAFT TYPE, MODEL & SERIES	NO. LANDINGS	FLYING INST. (INCL IN 1ST PIL. TIME) S	COMMD. PILOT C CA	CO. PILOT CP	QUALI- FIED PILOT DUAL QD	FIRST PILOT DAY F	FIRST PILOT NIGHT F N OR NI	RATED PERS. NON-PILOT		NON-RATED OTHER ARMS & SERVICES	NON-RATED OTHER CREW & PASS GR	SPECIAL INFORMATION INSTRU- MENT I	NIGHT N	INSTRU- MENT TRAINER	PILOT NON-MIL. AIRCRAFT MIL.	NON- MIL.
15	19	20	21	22	23	24	25	26	27	28 29	30	31	32	33	34	35	36
1	B-24J	1										1:00					
2	B-24J	1										3:50					
12	B-24J	1										4:55					
16	B-24J	1										7:00	6:00				
17	B-24J	1										5:45					
19	B-24J	1										6:10					
20	B-24J	1										3:55					

Leaving the ZI for 451st B. Group
Castelluccio, Italy

CERTIFIED CORRECT:

Henry B. Hard

HENRY B. HARD
1st Lt., Air Corps,
Operations Officer.

This month
Prev months
Totals to date

COLUMN TOTALS   33:35   6:00 Non

	[42] TOTAL STUDENT PILOT TIME	[43] TOTAL FIRST PILOT TIME	[44] TOTAL PILOT TIME
(37) THIS MONTH Comb at Tr			33:35
(38) PREVIOUS MONTHS THIS F. Y.			142:15
(39) THIS FISCAL YEAR			175:50
(40) PREVIOUS FISCAL YEARS			
(41) TO DATE			175:50

AIRCRAFT	NL	CARD NO. 1						CARD NO. 2					CARD NO. 3			
19	20 21	22	23	24	25	26	27	28	29	30	31	32	33	34	35	

AAF FORM 202, 5
APPROVED DEC. 7, 1943

INDIVIDUAL FLIGHT RECORD

(1) SERIAL NO. **31430427**　(2) NAME **Kozakis**　**Achilles**　**NMI**　(3) RANK **Cpl**　(4) AGE
(5) PERS. CLASS ____　(6) BRANCH **Air Corps**　(7) STATION **APO 520**
(8) ORGANIZATION ASSIGNED **15th** AIR FORCE　**49th** WING　**451st** GROUP　**726th** SQUADRON　ATTACHED FOR FLYING
(9) ORGANIZATION ATTACHED ____ AIR FORCE　COMMAND　WING　GROUP　SQUADRON　DETACHMENT
(10) PRESENT RATING & DATE ____　(11) ORIGINAL RATING & DATE ____
(12) TRANSFERRED FROM ____　(13) FLIGHT RESTRICTIONS ____
(15) TRANSFERRED TO ____　(14) TRANSFER DATE ____

(16) PERS CLASS	RANK	RTG	A. F.	COMMAND	WING	GROUP NO.	TYPE	SQUADRON NO.	TYPE	STATION	MQ	YR	(17) MONTH November 19 44

DAY	AIRCRAFT TYPE, MODEL & SERIES	NO. LANDINGS	FLYING INST. (INCL IN 1ST PIL TIME) S	COMMD. PILOT C CA	CO-PILOT CP	QUALI-FIED PILOT DUAL QD	FIRST PILOT DAY P	FIRST PILOT NIGHT P N OR NI	RATED PERS. NON-PILOT			NON-RATED OTHER ARMS & SERVICES	NON-RATED OTHER CREW & PASS GP	INSTRU-MENT I	NIGHT N	INSTRU-MENT TRAINER	PILOT NON-MIL AICRAFT 450 HP 400 N	
18	19	20	21	22	23	24	25	26	27	28	29	30	31	32	33	34	35	36
5	B-24J	1											4:00				1	
6	B-24J	1											7:30				1	
12	B-24J	1											3:00					
13	B-24J	1											2:10					
16	B-24G	1											7:30					
17	B-24G	1											8:00				1	
18	B-24J	1			5 Consecutive Days								6:00				1	
19	B-24H	1											7:00				1	
20	B-24J	1											9:00				1	
24	B-24J	1											3:15					
26	B-24J	1											1:50					
													59:15					

CERTIFIED CORRECT:

Henry B. Ford

HENRY B. FORD,
1st Lt., Air Corps,
Operations Officer.

This month	7
Prev months	
Totals to date	7

| COLUMN TOTALS | | | | | | | | | | | | | 59:15 | | | | Non |

	(42) TOTAL STUDENT PILOT TIME	(43) TOTAL FIRST PILOT TIME	(44) TOTAL PILOT TIME
(37) THIS MONTH			59:15
(38) PREVIOUS MONTHS THIS F. Y.			175:50
(39) THIS FISCAL YEAR			235:05
(40) PREVIOUS FISCAL YEARS			
(41) TO DATE			235:05

AIRCRAFT	NL	CARD NO. 1						CARD NO. 2					CARD NO. 3				
19	20	21	22	23	24	25	26	27	28	29	30	31	32	33	34	35	36

INDIVIDUAL FLIGHT RECORD

(1) SERIAL NO. 31430127 (2) NAME Kozakis Achilles (3) RANK S/Sgt (4) AGE
(5) PERS. CLASS (6) BRANCH Air Corps (7) STATION APO 520
(8) ORGANIZATION ASSIGNED 15th 49th 61st 720th
(9) ORGANIZATION ATTACHED AIR FORCE COMMAND WING GROUP SQUADRON
(10) PRESENT RATING & DATE (11) ORIGINAL RATING & DATE
(12) TRANSFERRED FROM (13) FLIGHT RESTRICTIONS
(15) TRANSFERRED TO (14) TRANSFER DATE

(16) PERS CLASS	RANK	RTG	A.F.	COMMAND	WING	GROUP NO.	GROUP TYPE	SQUADRON NO.	SQUADRON TYPE	STATION	MO.	YR.	(17) MONTH December 19 44

DAY	AIRCRAFT TYPE, MODEL & SERIES	NO. LANDINGS	FLYING INST. INCL IN 1ST MIL. TIME	COMMD. PILOT C CA	CO. PILOT CP	QUALIFIED PILOT DUAL QD	FIRST PILOT DAY P	FIRST PILOT NIGHT P N OR NI	RATED PERS. NON-PILOT			NON-RATED OTHER ARMS & SERVICES	NON-RATED OTHER CREW & PASS'GR	INSTRUMENT I	NIGHT N	INSTRUMENT TRAINER	PILOT NON-MIL. AIRCRAFT OVER 400 H.P.	PILOT NON-MIL. AIRCRAFT UNDER 400 H.P.
18	19	20	21	22	23	24	25	26	27	28	29	30	31	32	33	34	35	36
3	B-24H	1											3:00	Combat	RC			
6	B-24H	1											6:45	Combat		8		
8	B-24J	1											2:00					
9	B-24J	1											2:25	Combat	ER			
15	B-24J	1											7:40	Combat		9		
16	B-24J	1											1:30	Combat	ER			
18	3-24J	1											4:45	Combat	ER			
20	B-24J	1											7:15	Combat		10		
25	B-24L	1			Christmas Day								8:00	Combat		11		
26	B-24J	1											8:30	Combat		12		
27	B-24J	1											5:30	Combat		13		

CERTIFIED CORRECT:

Henry B. Ford

HENRY B. FORD,
Captain, Air Corps,
Operations Officer.

| COLUMN TOTALS | | | | | | | | | | | | | 55:20 | | Non | | | |

	(42) TOTAL STUDENT PILOT TIME	(43) TOTAL FIRST PILOT TIME	(44) TOTAL PILOT TIME
(37) THIS MONTH			55:20
(38) PREVIOUS MONTHS THIS F. Y.			235:05
(39) THIS FISCAL YEAR			290:25
(40) PREVIOUS FISCAL YEARS			
(41) TO DATE			290:25

AIRCRAFT 19	NL 20	CARD NO. 1 21	22	23	24	25	26	CARD NO. 2 27	28	29	30	31	CARD NO. 3 32	33	34	35	36

(DIVIDUAL FLIGHT RECC)

(1)SERIAL NO. 31430427 (2)NAME Kozakis Achilles (3)RANK S/Sgt. (4)AGE
(5) PERS. CLASS (6)BRANCH Air Corps (7)STATION APC 520
(8) ORGANIZATION ASSIGNED 461st 726th 15th 49th
(9) ORGANIZATION ATTACHED
(10)PRESENT RATING & DATE (11)ORIGINAL RATING & DATE
(12) TRANSFERRED FROM (13)FLIGHT RESTRICTIONS
(15) TRANSFERRED TO (14) TRANSFER DATE

(16) PERS CLASS	RANK	RTG.	A.F.	COMMAND	WING	GROUP NO.	TYPE	SQUADRON NO.	TYPE	STATION	MO.	YR.	(17) MONTH January 19

DAY	AIRCRAFT TYPE, MODEL & SERIES	NO. LANDINGS	FLYING INST. (INCL IN 1ST PIL. TIME) S	COMMD. PILOT C CA	CO-PILOT CP	QUALI-FIED PILOT DUAL QD	FIRST PILOT DAY P	NIGHT P. N OR NI	RATED PERS. NON-PILOT			OTHER ARMS & SERVICES	OTHER CREW & PASS'GR	INSTRU-MENT I	NIGHT N	INSTRU-MENT TRAINER	PILOT NON AIRCRA OVER 400 M.P.
18	19	20	21	22	23	24	25	26	27	28	29	30	31	32	33	34	35
5	B-24L	1											5:45		14		Comba
20	B-24L	1											6:50		15		Comba

15th Air Force Grounded because of bad weather.

451ST Flew 5 missions this month!

CERTIFIED CORRECT:

HENRY R. FORD,
CAPTAIN, AIR CORPS,
OPERATIONS OFFICER.

| COLUMN TOTALS | | | | | | | | | | | | | | 12:35 | | NON | |

	(42) TOTAL STUDENT PILOT TIME	(43) TOTAL FIRST PILOT TIME	(44) TOTAL PILOT TIME
(37) THIS MONTH			12:35
(38) PREVIOUS MONTHS THIS F. Y.			290:25
(39) THIS FISCAL YEAR			313:00
(40) PREVIOUS FISCAL YEARS			
(41) TO DATE			313:00

AIRCRAFT	NL	CARD NO. 1						CARD NO. 2					CARD NO. 3			
19	20	21	22	23	24	25	26	27	28	29	30	31	32	33	34	35

DIVIDUAL FLIGHT RECC D

(1) SERIAL NO. **31430427** (2) NAME **Kozakis** **Achilles** (3) RANK **S/Sgt** (4) AGE

(5) PERS. CLASS **38** (6) BRANCH **Air Corps** (7) STATION **APO 520**

(8) ORGANIZATION ASSIGNED **15th** **49th** **461st** **726th**

(9) ORGANIZATION ATTACHED

(10) PRESENT RATING & DATE _____ (11) ORIGINAL RATING & DATE

(12) TRANSFERRED FROM _____ (13) FLIGHT RESTRICTIONS

(15) TRANSFERRED TO _____ (14) TRANSFER DATE

(17) MONTH **February** 19 4

DAY	AIRCRAFT TYPE, MODEL & SERIES	NO. LANDINGS	FLYING INST. (INCL IN 1ST PL TIME) S	COMMD. PILOT C CA	CO-PILOT CP	QUALIFIED PILOT DUAL QD	FIRST PILOT DAY P	NIGHT P N OR NI	NON-PILOT 27	28	29	OTHER ARMS & SERVICES 30	OTHER CREW & PASS'GR 31	INSTRUMENT 1	NIGHT N	INSTRUMENT TRAINER	OVER 400 H.P.	UND'R 400 H	SPECIAL INFORMATION
1	B-24J	1											1	8:00						Combat
7	B-24L	1											1	7:45						Combat
14	B-24L	1											1	7:45						Combat
18	B-24L	1												3:30						Combat R
20	B-24L	1											1	6:15						Combat
22	B-24L	1											1	8:15						Combat
28	B-24L	1											1	7:30						Combat

CERTIFIED CORRECT:

Charles W. Atterholt

CHARLES W. ATTERHOLT,
Captain, Air Corps,
Operations Officer.

This mo 6
Prev mo 15
Totals 21

COLUMN TOTALS 49:00 **Non**

	(42) TOTAL STUDENT PILOT TIME	(43) TOTAL FIRST PILOT TIME	(44) TOTAL PILOT TIME
(37) THIS MONTH **Combat Hrs**	49:00		49:00
(38) PREVIOUS MONTHS THIS F.Y.	116:25		313:00
(39) THIS FISCAL YEAR	165:25		362:00
(40) PREVIOUS FISCAL YEARS			
(41) TO DATE			362:00

	AIRCRAFT	NL	CARD NO. 1						CARD NO. 2				CARD NO. 3			
	19	20	21	22	23	24	25	26	27	28	29	30	31	32	33	34	35

INDIVIDUAL FLIGHT RECORD

(1) SERIAL NO. 31430427   (2) NAME **Kozakis**   **Achilles**   (3) RANK **S/Sgt**   (4) AGE 19 23
(5) PERS. CLASS **38**   (6) BRANCH **Air Corps**   (7) STATION **APO 520**
(8) ORGANIZATION ASSIGNED **15th**   **49th**   **451st**   **728th**
(9) ORGANIZATION ATTACHED
(10) PRESENT RATING & DATE **Gunner**   (11) ORIGINAL RATING & DATE
(12) TRANSFERRED FROM   (13) FLIGHT RESTRICTIONS **None**
(15) TRANSFERRED TO   (14) TRANSFER DATE

(17) MONTH **March** 1 **45**

DAY	AIRCRAFT TYPE, MODEL & SERIES	LANDINGS	FLYING INST (HRS) IN 1ST PIL FINAL	COMMD. PILOT C CA	CO. PILOT CP	QUAL'D & 2ND PILOT DUAL '2S'	FIRST PILOT DAY	FIRST PILOT NIGHT P N OR NI	RATED PERS. NON-PILOT		NON-RATED OTHER ARMS & SERVICES	NON-RATED OTHER CREW & PASS'GR	INSTRU- MENT	NIGHT N	INSTRU- MENT TRAINER	PILOT NON-M AIRCRAFT OVER 400 H.P. GND 400
2	B-24L	1									1	6:00				Combat
4	B-24L	1									1	7:30				Combat
21	B-24J	1									1	7:30				Combat
26	B-24J	1									1	8:30				Combat

Rest Camp - Isle of Capri
April 5th — 19th

Charles W. Atterholt
Captain, Air Corps,
Operations Officer.

This no	4
Prev no	21
Totals	25

| COLUMN TOTALS | | | | | | | | | | | | 31:30 | | | Non |

	(42) TOTAL STUDENT PILOT TIME	(43) TOTAL FIRST PILOT TIME	(44) TOTAL PILOT TIME
(37) THIS MONTH **Combat yrs**	31:30		31:30
(38) PREVIOUS MONTHS THIS F.Y.	165:25		362:00
(39) THIS FISCAL YEAR	196:55		393:30
(40) PREVIOUS FISCAL YEARS			
(41) TO DATE			393:30

	AIRCRAFT	NL	CARD NO. 1						CARD NO. 2				CARD NO. 3			
	19	20 21	22	23	24	25	26	27	28	29	30	31	32	33	34	35	36

AAF FORM NO. 5
APPROVED DEC. 7, 1942

INDIVIDUAL FLIGHT RECORD

(1) SERIAL NO. **31430427** (2) NAME **KOZAKIS   ACHILLES**   MIDDLE   (3) RANK **S/Sgt.** (4) AGE **19 23**

(5) PERS. CLASS **38** (6) BRANCH **Air Corps** (7) STATION **APO 520**   ATTACHED FOR FLYING

(8) ORGANIZATION ASSIGNED **15th**   AIR FORCE   **49th**   COMMAND   **451st**   WING   **726th**   GROUP   SQUADRON   DETACHMENT

(9) ORGANIZATION ATTACHED

(10) PRESENT RATING & DATE **Gunner (612)** (11) ORIGINAL RATING & DATE **same**

(12) TRANSFERRED FROM   (13) FLIGHT RESTRICTIONS **none**

(15) TRANSFERRED TO   (14) TRANSFER DATE

(16) PERS CLASS	RANK	RTG.	A. F.	COMMAND	WING	GROUP NO.	TYPE	SQUADRON NO.	TYPE	STATION	MO.	YR.	(17) MONTH **April** 19 **45**
:	:	:	:	:	:	:	:	:	:	:	:	:	

DAY	AIRCRAFT TYPE, MODEL & SERIES	NO. LANDINGS	FLYING INST. (INCL IN 1ST PIL TIME) S	COMMD. PILOT C CA	CO-PILOT CP	QUALI-FIED PILOT DUAL QD	FIRST PILOT DAY P	FIRST PILOT NIGHT P N OR NI	RATED PERS. NON-PILOT 27	28	29	NON-RATED OTHER ARMS & SERVICES 18	OTHER CREW & PASS'GR 31	INSTRU-MENT T	NIGHT N	INSTRU-MENT TRAINER	PILOT NON-MIL AIRCRAFT OVER 400 M.P.	UNDER 400 H.
18	19	20	21	22	23	24	25	26	27	28	29	30	31	32	33	34	35	36
2	B-24L	1										1	7:00				Combat	
5	B-24L	1										1	5:45				Combat	
7	B-24L	1		Did not drop bombs									5:20				Combat	
8	B-24J	1		Did not drop bombs									4:40				Combat	
9	B-24J	1		Invasion of the Po Valley		Brit. 8th Army						1	5:00				Combat	
10	B-24M	1		DH	"	"						1	4:45				Combat	
19	B-24L	1										1	7:00				Combat	
20	B-24L	1										1	6:30				Combat	
21	B-24G	1										1	7:00				Combat	
23	B-24J	1										1	6:15				Combat	
24	B-24L	1										1	7:00				Combat	
25	B-24L	1										1 1 0	7:45			:|	Combat	

CERTIFIED CORRECT:

Charles W. Attuholt

CHARLES W. ATTUHOLT,
Captain, Air Corps,
Operations Officer.

This mo	10		
Prev mo	25		
Totals	35		

COLUMN TOTALS: 74:00   Non

	(42) TOTAL STUDENT PILOT TIME	(43) TOTAL FIRST PILOT TIME	(44) TOTAL PILOT TIME
(37) THIS MONTH **Combat Hrs**	6:40 **54:00**		**74:00**
(38) PREVIOUS MONTHS THIS F. Y.	**196:55**		**393:30**
(39) THIS FISCAL YEAR	**250:55**		**467:30**
(40) PREVIOUS FISCAL YEARS			**467:30**
(41) TO DATE			

	AIRCRAFT	NL	CARD NO. 1						CARD NO. 2					CARD NO. 3			
DO NOT WRITE IN THIS SPACE	19	20	21	22	23	24	25	26	27	28	29	30	31	32	33	34	35	36

IN DIVIDUAL FLIGHT RECORD

(1) SERIAL NO. 31430427   (2) NAME ROGERS   ACHILLES   (3) RANK. S/Sgt   (4) AGE 1923
          LAST   FIRST   MIDDLE

(5) PERS. CLASS 38   (6) BRANCH Air Corps   (7) STATION APC 520
          AIR FORCE   ATTACHED FOR FLYING

(8) ORGANIZATION ASSIGNED 15th   49th   451st   728th
          AIR FORCE   COMMAND   WING   GROUP   SQUADRON   DETACHMENT

(9) ORGANIZATION ATTACHED

(10) PRESENT RATING & DATE Gunner 621   (11) ORIGINAL RATING & DATE Same

(12) TRANSFERRED FROM   (13) FLIGHT RESTRICTIONS None

(15) TRANSFERRED TO   (14) TRANSFER DATE

(16)
DO NOT WRITE IN THIS SPACE

PERS CLASS	RANK	RTG.	A. F.	COMMAND	WING	GROUP NO.	GROUP TYPE	SQUADRON NO.	SQUADRON TYPE	STATION	MO.	YR.	(17) MONTH May 19 45

DAY	AIRCRAFT TYPE, MODEL & SERIES	NO. LANDINGS	FLYING INST. (INCL IN 1ST PIL TIME) S	COMMD. PILOT C CA	CO-PILOT CP	QUALI-FIED PILOT DUAL GO	FIRST PILOT DAY P	FIRST PILOT NIGHT F N OR NI	RATED PERS. NON-PILOT P	RATED PERS. 28	RATED PERS. 29	NON-RATED OTHER ARMS & SERVICES	NON-RATED OTHER CREW & PASS'GR	SPECIAL INFORMATION INSTRU-MENT I	NIGHT N	INSTRU-MENT TRAINER	PILOT NON-MIL. AIRCRAFT OVER 400 H.P.	PILOT NON-MIL. AIRCRAFT UNDER 400 H.P.
18	19	20	21	22	23	24	25	26	27	28	29	30	31	32	33	34	35	36
									NO FLYING TIME THIS MONTH - MISSIONS COMPLETED									
									CERTIFIED CORRECT:						Finito!!			
									Charles W. Atterholt									
									CHARLES W. ATTERHOLT,									
									Captain, Air Corps,									
									Operations Officer.									
									CLOSED OUT - Change of Station									
															Home Sweet Home			
COLUMN TOTALS																NON		

	(42) TOTAL STUDENT PILOT TIME	(43) TOTAL FIRST PILOT TIME	(44) TOTAL PILOT TIME
(37) THIS MONTH Combat Hours			
(38) PREVIOUS MONTHS THIS F. Y.	260:55		467:30
(39) THIS FISCAL YEAR	260:55		467:30
(40) PREVIOUS FISCAL YEARS			
(41) TO DATE			467:30

	AIRCRAFT	NL	CARD NO. 1						CARD NO. 2					CARD NO. 3				
DO NOT WRITE IN THIS SPACE	19	20	21	22	23	24	25	26	27	28	29	30	31	32	33	34	35	36

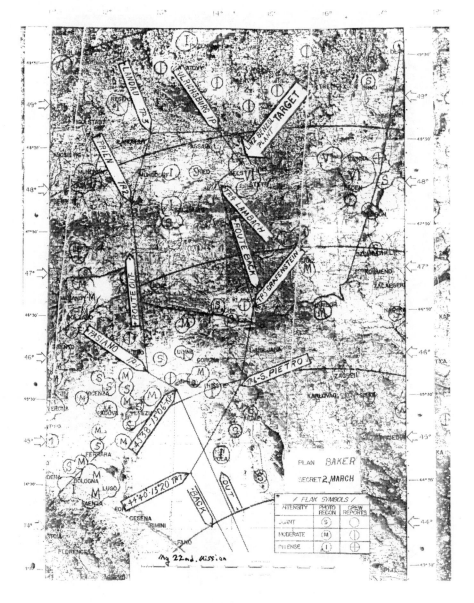

My 22nd Mission

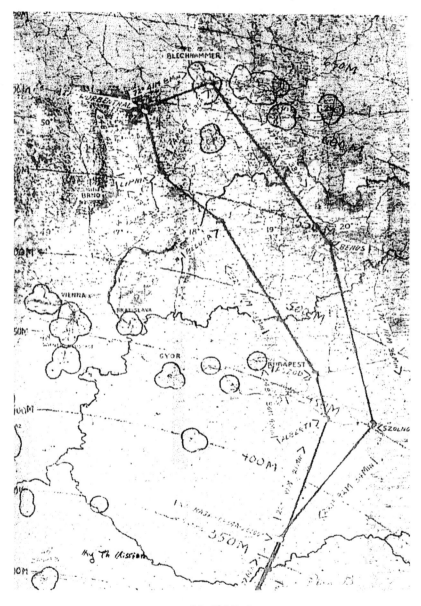

My 7th Mission

PLAN ABLE   5 January 1945.

TARGET: ZAGREB EXTREME WEST SIDINGS (4549N 1555E) Axis: 56° Rally: Shp Loft
       Bombing Altitude: 25,000 Tgt Elev: 400 plus or minus 50 ft.
       Area to be bombed: See annotated photo.
       IP: Ozalj (4537N 1529E)   Target time: 1050.
NO ALTERNATES:
KEY POINT: Zirge (4339N 1540E) 19,000 ft at 1006.
TAKE-OFF: 0735   DEPART BASE: 0852 at 13,000   ETR: 1235

FLAK ENROUTE: Lussinpiccolo (4432N 1428E)   Fiume (4520N 1428E)
                Karlovac (4530N 1532E)   Sisak (4530N 1622E)

MAPS USED: OFF
         Naples   4220N 1519E
        Chiéti   4420N 1523E   Graz - Firenze - Venezia
        Fiume   4400N 1513E

FLIGHT PLAN:	DIST	MC	DC	AV ALT	TAS	GS	TIME	ETA
Depart Bovino at 0916 at 13,000								
Casalnuovo	25	333	-11	13000	169	156	:10	0926
KP Zirge (4339N 1540E)	125	012	-10	16000	177	188	:40	1006
TP #1 Dreznica (4508N 1506E)	92	344	-11	23000	199	206	:27	1033
IP Ozalj (4537N 1529E)	33	030	-7	25000	205	235	:08	1041
Target (4549N 1555E)	25	056	-2	25000	205	245	:06	1047
TP #1 Dreznica (4508N 1506E)	55	222	+5	24000	202	165	:20	1107
Base	229	175	+12	12000	166	159	1:26	1233

WINDS USED IN FLIGHT PLAN:
Base   6,000 ft   267 deg   22 knots   -5 5   226/20
        8,000 ft   264 deg   26 knots   -10 10   230/30
      10,000 ft   260 deg   30 knots   -15 15   230/40
      12,000 ft   260 deg   33 knots   -12 15   230/40
      14,000 ft   260 deg   35 knots   -17   220/45
      16,000 ft   260 deg   38 knots   -20 20
Route   14,000 ft   252 deg   35 knots   -18 25   220/50
      16,000 ft   248 deg   35 knots   -22
      20,000 ft   240 deg   35 knots   -29   220/45
      22,000 ft   244 deg   37 knots   -33   230/50
      24,000 ft   248 deg   39 knots   -37
      26,000 ft   252 deg   42 knots   -42
Target   22,000   244 deg   37 knots   -33
      24,000 ft   248 deg   39 knots   -38
      26,000 ft   252 deg   42 knots   -43
      28,000 ft   256 deg   43 knots   -47

*Given to me by My
(1st. Lt. Burton Schilling), Lead Navigator
on My 14th. Mission*

32+

12000

THE B-DASH TWO FOUR
****

DOWN IN FLAK VALLEY WHERE THE BLACK MUSHROOM GROW
THE 451ST AND THEIR BIG BOMBERS GO;
WE'RE BRIEFED IN THE MORNING AND TOLD THERE IS NO FLAK
WE FLY DOWN THAT VALLEY AND NEVER COME BACK.

CHORUS

OH THAT B DASH TWO FOUR.
OH THAT FOUR ENGINE WHORE.
THE BOYS WHO FLY IN HER ARE SURE BOUND TO LOSE;
AT FIFTY-FIVE INCHES SHE WON'T EVEN CRUISE.
OH THAT B DASH TWO FOUR.

THE C.Q. AWAKES US AT ONE-FORTY-FIVE
WE GO TO THE BRIEFING AND WHEN WE ARRIVE,
WE'RE GOING TO PLOESTI, THE FIFTH TIME THIS WEEK.
WE'RE SCARED TO FLY OVER THE TARGET WE SEEK.

WE'RE TOLD THE WEATHER IS C-A-V-U,
BUT WE CAN'T SEE THE GROUND AT 100 FEET TRUE;
THREE LAYERS OF CLOUDS HIDE THE EARTH FROM THE SKY,
TO CLEAR ALL THE WEATHER WE'VE GOT TO FLY HIGH.

WE RENDEZVOUS OVER THE ISLE OF CAPRI
AND WE WONDER WHEREVER OUR MUSTANGS CAN BE
THEN OFF TO THE TARGET WITHOUT AN ESCORT,
ONE LOOK AT THAT VALLEY AND WISE MEN ABORT.

WE TAKE OFF FOR FRANCE WITH A FULL LOAD OF GAS.
IF WE LOSE AN ENGINE IT WILL BE OUR ASS.
NINE HOURS OF FORMATION, THE MISSION COUNTS ONE,
NO FLAK, NO FIGHTERS, NO DAMAGE TO THE HUN.

WE LOOK AT THE GROUND THROUGH A POWERFUL GLASS.
AND WE SEE ALL THE HUNS SHOOTING SKEET IN THE GRASS;
THE RESULTS ARE ALL HORRID, ITS ALWAYS THE SAME,
AS FOOLISH YOUNG MOTH FLYING INTO A FLAME.

WE FEATHERED A FAN O'ER VIENNA ONE DAY,
WE CALLED FOR THE GROUP, BUT THEY'D ALL GONE AWAY;
LEFT TO THE MERCY OF FIGHTERS AND FLAK,
IT'S A HELLUVA WONDER WE EVER GOT BACK.

THE COLONEL'S AND MAJOR'S THE MILK RUNS DO FLY,
THEY SEND US TO TARGETS WHERE MANY MEN DIE.
BUT JUST ABOUT THE TIME THEY CRAWL OUT OF THE SACK,
WE'VE FEATHERED A FAN AND WE'RE ON THE WAY BACK.

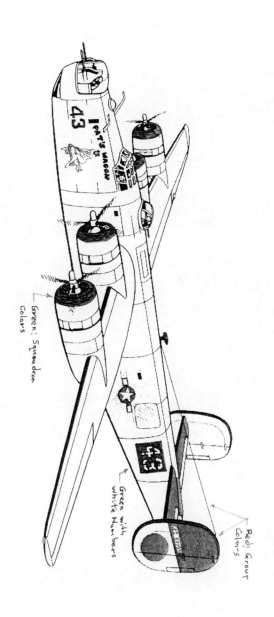

"As Flak Goes By"

You must remember this, that flak doesn't — *Anti-aircraft shrapnel*
always miss
Somebody's got to die.
The fundamental things apply as flak goes
by.

And when the fighters come, you pray
you're not the one
To tumble from the sky.
You wish you had a quart of rye as flak ← *"2 ounces of 100 proof Rye for each Crewman given after each Mission."*
goes by.

One ten's and two ten's *come* a-knocking' at ← *German Fighter-Interceptor Aircraft (Twin Engine)*
~~your the~~ gate,
The sky is full of tracers; I've got to kill my
rate.
Open the bomb bays, salvo—don't *you* wait;
The Target's rushing by.

It's still the same old story, the 8th gets all ← *Glorified 8th Air Force based in England.*
the glory
While we go out and die......
The odds are always too damned high, as
flak goes by.

You must remember this, that flak doesn't
always miss
Somebody's got to die.
The fundamental things apply as flak goes
by.

Editor's Note: The above is a parody of the song "AS TIME GOES BY," from the movie "Casablanca." Remember Humphrey "Boggie" Bogart telling Sam to "play it again?" While the author is unknown, this little song said a lot about the fact that the 8th Air Force got the lion's share of the publicity, while the groups of the 15th fought the same war and got very little credit.

451st BOMB GROUP (H) LTD. , WW-2

1032 S. State Street Marengo, IL 60152

FAX Message

Ph. (815) 568-7766 .... **FAX (815) 568-0451**

Date: DEC 2 2 1997

Achi;

Amid the ringing of doorbells, scurrying of dogs, and the shuffling of aging feet, I was greeted at my door by the "DHL" express mail deliver'er this morning. In her hands was the promised packet that I eagerly awaited. Waving her a fond farewell, and blowing her a kiss, I retired into my living room where I anxiously went through the material you had sent.

My first impression upon opening was: ... "My God, those flak towers were much bigger than I had ever imagined!" Not necessarily in height but in girth. As seen from the air they appeared much smaller; not that I paid particular attention to dimensions, but rather gave close attention to the muzzle blasts that always appeared to be aimed at me. What I would ask of you, in using these pictures in the next newsletter, could you loan me the originals? I can have them 1/2 toned (for printing purposes) much cheaper in smaller format.

As an aside, did you know that the Germans were using children from the ages of 12 up as "carriers and loaders" at some flak gun emplacements? I had a book sent to me by an Austrian author that I had befriended and it gave a good accounting of this fact. Trouble was that I loaned it to a German girl that I was going with at the time (for translation purposes only - TRUTH!) and she couldn't seem to find it at the time of our break-up. I was tempted to ask the author for another copy, but since I don't understand nor read German I figured it was a lost cause.

As to the much touted "Ploesti Picture," anyone can take all the liberties they want with the "Dersh Painting," as it only represents a generic version of the actual photo. And since Mr. Dersh is deceased, and it wasn't copyright protected, anyone has legal rights to the use of it. At least that's what I heard coming down from the "grapevine."

Now that you explained and displayed the "Silver Bell," I remember them! I never owned one, but I remember them. When I have some time after the New Year, I'll try and make contact with the Federico family on Capri.

Until later, Achi, YOU and your family have a wonderful Holiday Season. I, nor the 451st, will ever forget your generous donations over this past year. Because of your generosity the BIG newsletter is "on it's way."

Bob Karstensen
(ONE OF YOUR BUDDIES)

TRIBUTE TO ALL 451ST PERSONNEL ... YET LIVING, OR IN THE HIGH FLIGHT

The Final Inspection
>
> The soldier stood and faced God
> Which must always come to pass
> He hoped his shoes were shining
> Just as brightly as his brass.
>
> "Step forward now, you soldier
> How shall I deal with you?
> Have you always turned the other cheek?
> To My Church have you been true?"
>
> The soldier squared his shoulders and said,
> "No, Lord, I guess I ain't
> Because those of us who carry guns
> Can't always be a saint.
>
> I've had to work most Sundays
> And at times my talk was tough,
> And sometimes I've been violent,
> Because the world is awfully rough.
>
> But, I never took a penny
> That wasn't mine to keep...
> Though I worked a lot of overtime
> When the bills got just too steep.
>
> And I never passed a cry for help,
> Though at times I shook with fear,
> And sometimes,
> God forgive me, I've wept unmanly tears.
>
> I know I don't deserve a place
> Among the people here,
> They never wanted me around
> Except to calm their fears.
>
> If you've a place for me here, Lord,
> It needn't be so grand,
> I never expected or had too much,
> But if you don't, I'll understand."
>
> There was a silence all around the throne
> Where the saints had often trod
> As the soldier waited quietly,
> For the judgment of his God,
>
> "Step forward now, you soldier,
> You've borne your burdens well,
> Walk peacefully on Heaven's streets,
> You've done your time in Hell."
>
> To all that serve

From: BobK451

FRIENDLY FIGHTER vs. FRIENDLY BOMBER

A P-51 and P-38 were escorting a B-24 and their pilots were chatting with each other to pass the time. Talk fell to the subject of the relative merits of their respective aircraft with the fighter pilots holding that their aircraft were better because of their maneuverability, weaponry and the like.

The B-24 pilot replied, "Yeah? Well I can do a few things with this old girl that you'd only dream about." Naturally he was challenged to demonstrate. "Just watch," he tells them.

The Bomber continues to fly straight and level and after several minutes the Liberator pilot returns to the air and says, "There! How was that?"

Not having seen anything, the Fighter pilots say, "What are you talking about? What did you do?"

He replies, "Well, I got up, stretched my legs, got a cup of coffee and went in the back and took a leak."

From: BobK451

03/12/99

Dear Achi & Rena,

Thank you so much for the great hat that you sent me. No one
has ever done anything like that for me before, and it fits great.
I've been having a little problem with my health and have been
Hospitalized for several days during Christmas week and was
released on the 4th of January. I'm doing much better now but
I have to go in on occasion as an out Patient to get shock
treatment in an effort to correct an irregular heartbeat they call
it Atrial Fibrilations.

Enough about me, your writing is great and it brings back
Memories, especially the Latrine routine and the 726th "Rec"
Room. We enjoyed all of your writing and I think you have
Talent. My brother is in process of writing a book and expects
To be finished with it in June of this year, its about our family &
friends when we were growing up along with some of his
experiences in WW II, he was in the Normandy invasion & the
Battle of the Bulge, where he was wounded & hospitalized for
Two & one half months.

It was nice that your boys went with you to the Reunion. I
Hope that I will make the next one in the year 2000 to see some

Joe Carmelo

Of our old friends & buddies. Achi, we had a mutual old friend Vince Demopoulos who has since died, that we both knew and were very fond of. He was an unforgettable person that did so much for our outfit, like spicing up C-ration stew to make it eatable. He was strictly business as the mess Sgt. And a delight to be around in our leisure time.

Achi, my wife Jeannette is an expert knitter & she has knitted a Pair of slippers for you & Rena and we hope you enjoy them, they ware great & last a long time. That's all I have for now & keep up with your writing and maybe it will find its way into a Book some day. I'm into art, Portraits, Horses & Scenery. My problem is that I can't stay motivated--think they call it old age. A better term for it is less young! Bye for now & may God Bless you and your family.   Sincerely,

Your fellow 451'er & 726'er   Joe

Joe

Achilles Kozakis
20011 Tilstock Dr
Katy, TX 77450-4345
(281) 579-3019

03 May 1999

Hello Joe & Jennette,

I just want you to know how much I appreciate your most interesting letter and the great slippers. Both found us in good health and in the best of spirits. The slippers are the perfect gift and I use them daily. We think about you everyday we wear them and they are truly a gift of tender loving care. Again thank you.

We are hopeful that your health will improve in time. The years are multiplying and our time on this earth is diminishing as days go by. Think positive, be positive and you shall continue to be my friend and buddy. I'm sure there are many of us who are handicapped in some manner. Personally, I have learned to take a day at a time and enjoy what I do. I'm looking froward to the 2000 reunion and I'll be looking for you - dear buddy.

I'm glad you mentioned our mutual friend, Demopoulos. It brought back a wonderful memory of an incident that occurred on Christmas day 1944. The night before, on Christmas Eve, we were told that our crew would not fly on Christmas because of bad weather. This was great news, of course. Too bad the promise only lasted until 0300 hrs Christmas day when we were wakened by the Sq'dn Operations clerk to prepare for the day's mission (synthetic rubber plant, Oswieci m, Poland). To shorten the story, it was a long, cold and hazardous mission. We arrived on base very late and the mess hall was closed. Of course, we were hungry and angry, but upon my visit to the kitchen, Vince Demopoulos listened to my plea (in half Greek, half English) and gave me a can of turkey to share with my crew. Thus, we had a Christmas turkey dinner. Joe, as you well know, it is comradeship like this that binds us together for the rest our lives.

Please keep me informed of your brother's book. I am happy to learn he is writing. Joe, I think you should write about the ground crews. The men who kept us flying and who toiled day and night, rain or shine!

NEXT WEEK WE'VE GOT TO GET ORGANIZED

Hey, how about some sketches or drawings of your experiences? Maybe we can collaborate and come up with some poop for the *"Ad Lib"*. Let me know how you feel about this.

Well dear buddy, I have to cut this short and run. You all will hear from me again soon. In the mean time, take care of yourselves, stay warm and may God bless you all.

Sincerely,

Achi

p.s. I have enclosed a "tid bit" that I wrote recently. Hopefully, it may renew some experiences of your youth.

Dec 23, 1995

Dear Ashi-a-Rue,

Ier We received your Christmas card today and needless to say, I was happy to hear from you. What message I have left takes me back 51 years when our crew stood for a Christmas day somewhere in Austria. That was supposed to be a milk run. They said a bunch of old ladies were shooting the guns. But after we got to the I.P., I heard that more come massage "Hose camera crew, Flak 120 look level". Well those old ladies did a pretty good job on us from those flinner all the new thoicy through "Rodriggyez, I can still hear Sarns blue (sic)

Will fully wp both are looking forward to our Rendezvoz (sic) next September. Merry Christmas to you and yours Ad until next year, "Ball gunner, over and out"

With best wishes

for the holidays and the coming year.

Lauren + Betty

Dear Archi'   12~4-08

Thanks much for your draft book. I just started reading it and it really brought back memories. It was an exciting time and, of course, dangerous. For us that survived it well, it matured us and gave us a new perspective on life – for the better. We really enjoyed the reunion. Pete Petersen was life-long friend.

Thanks again and have a great holiday period.

Dear Schuller,

I read your manuscript completely – it brought back many memories. It improves your mission level with every event I read. It on of the more missions unrolating first-hand.

Hope we'll become – will. At God, it began to look a lot of work.

Best wishes

wishing your continued

Alex Pa

Letters to George

*Note: After 50 years of searching, thanks to the Internet I found George.

March 19, 1995

Hello George,

It was a pleasant surprise talking to you and learning you are retired and in good health and in good spirits. I am well and enjoying my work. However, I still have a sinus problem with al little touch of asthma now and then. I have learned to control and abate this problem with medication.

Well, where do we begin? I guess it's best to start where we left off. "Time waits for no one" and 50 years have past since we saw each other in Castelluccio. After spending 10 months in three Army General Hospitals, I was discharged in May 1946.

January '47, I was on my way to the University at Tucson, Arizona and I stopped over in Houston, Texas for a couple of days. Interestingly, I'm still on my way to Arizona! Some stop over, huh? Instead of moving on, I attended the University of Houston, met my wife Rena (a fellow student) in '48 (we've been married since) raised our family, four boys and two girls. Together, we've seen and have had our share of laughter, tears, good times & bad. We wouldn't change a thing if we had to do it over again. I'm sure you & Dorothy feel the same way.

After four years of schooling, the following 34 (+) years were spent working as Engineer (mech/elec) for several Consulting firms and lastly with the National Steel Corp. Since 1975, my partner "Skipper" Joffrion and I have been practicing Architecture & Engineering. During the past 20 years we grew into a Design & Build (turnkey) company. Most of our work has been located in the Middle East, North Africa and the Philippines. Of course, when the "oil patch" went dry during the late 80's, our business went 'south', as did many other oil exploration service companies.

Overseas turnkey projects demanded most of my time but Rena and I would meet in Europe and other places for a Holiday together, for a couple of weeks at a time, when the opportunity would present itself. This 'R&R' gave us the opportunity to see most of Europe and other interesting places. Most importantly though, we were together.

I have learned many things during my travels and one item stands out among them. That is, "the special interest groups" still control this world. However, as Gen. Patton once said, "You read their book, then you beat them at their own game!!" I may have not beaten them yet, but it was fun trying and I'm still trying!

It looks like I'll be visiting the Middle East again very soon. Some one has to rebuild the devastated areas and it's going to be challenge for everyone participating. As in the past, the adrenaline builds up and you're ready for the next mission.

I've given you a some background about my past, now it's your turn. Take time and drop me a few lines. I'm all eyes and ears and I'm looking forward to your letter. Hopefully, you'll include a photo or two.

George, the few moments we spent talking on the phone, brought back many wonderful days. Be it Capri, Naples or in combat, it was always a secured feeling knowing you had a buddy to rely on.

You may have gained a few pounds (and who hasn't?) since our last meeting. The copies of my passport photos will indicate the aging process of these past 49 years. As you will note, I did gain a little weight myself. The enclosed photos are for your keeping. I hope you will enjoy them as I have.

Best wishes to you & Dorothy.

Sincerely,

Achi

Achi
(pronounced "Aki")

My home address and telephone numbers follow:

20011 Tilstock Drive
Katy, Texas 77450-4346
Tel: 713.579.3019

p.s.   All rosters for Army & Army Air Force units for the years 1944 through 1946 were destroyed in the fire of the National Personnel Records Center located in St. Louis, Mo.

25 March 1995

Hello George,

It took some time to gather and assemble the attached data from my files, but I hope you'll find some of it interesting.

The following are highlights of my final year in the Army Air Corps. It answers the question of "What happened to A. Kozakis?"

On the 25th of April 1945, I completed my 35th mission, thus also completing my tour of overseas duty. As you may remember, we flew as a Lead Crew to Linz, Austria (marshalling yards). The 727th squadron was leading the "Group" for this mission and our crew lead "Flight B".

Pat was trying to persuade me to fly a *milk run (that would follow) instead of my last mission. Being a stubborn Greek, ¹I chose to complete my tour with our Crew. You may remember on that day, only two men from our squadron completed their missions. They were Moe (Morris) & Kozakis. The following day however, 48 men finished their tour and of course, it was a "milk run" (I don't blame them).

On or about May 10th, two days after the war had ended in Europe, I flew to Naples and arrived at an Embarkation Center. We completed processing and briefing and then proceeded to wait for a ship to take us stateside.

During this waiting period of a week to ten days, all personnel at the Center were required to pull some "minor detail". One day I was selected to be the "Mess Sgt.". Of course, I knew nothing about cooking. However, the Duty Master Sgt. explained it to me this way, as I confronted him about my detail. He said, "You're Greek aren't you?" "Yes Sarg", I retorted. "Well then, you're the Mess Sgt. for the day". Nothing more was said. I did my job for the day seeing that all men were fed. A most interesting and educational detail.

On the 21st of May, plus or minus, twenty-eight enlisted crew men and one Lt. Col. from various squadrons, boarded a Liberty Ship in Naples harbor. Several thousand other airmen boarded various ships anchored in the harbor. We learned our ship took only twenty-eight men because we were all from the Boston area. This convoy of approximately twenty ships was the last convoy to leave Naples. At Oran, Algeria, the convoy increased to some 46 ships of all flags. By the time we crossed the Azores (about four days later) the convoy was dispersed and all ships continued to their destinations at various speeds and directions. At this juncture, it was learned that all nearby enemy submarines were accounted for and were no longer threatening the convoy.

*The Squadron would allow aircrew men to fly milk runs for their last mission.
¹I answered Pat by saying "I began my tour of duty with you and I will complete my tour of duty with you"

We spent the following three weeks on board as "leisure tourists". Good food, good men and lots of sack time. But best of all, the ship was headed for New York Harbor!!

We arrived at approximately 1600 hours and because of our delayed arrival, we were to anchor for the night and wait for our bus until morning. No one was allowed to leave the ship except the Lt. Col. He took off for about four hours but then returned with newspapers and magazines for the air crew men on board. The sights and sounds of lower Manhattan and the harbor were overwhelming. City lights were on for the first time after the war ended. Incoming troop ships would be met by tug boats, flying flags, fire boats (blaring their horns), and water sprays made by their huge fire pumps. It was awesome.

Since we ate the same food as the merchant marines and the two Navy Gun crews, it was appropriate for the air crew men to give the ship's cook a "kitty" of some 600 dollars. The contribution was insignificant compared to the wonderful and delicious meals he served us. Besides, most of the money was donated from the "crap" games played on board.

The following morning, at approximately 0930 hrs., we docked on the Jersey side of New York harbor. You may have guessed we were the first troop ship to have arrived at this particular dock. Within minutes, the dock side was immersed with girls from neighboring buildings. To our surprise and satisfaction, we became their heroes for the next two hours as we waited for the bus to Camp Kilmer.

We arrived at Camp Kilmer at approximately 1430 hrs. and proceeded with processing and had our first stateside steak dinner with all the ice cream and soda we could stand. Later that evening the twenty-eight men and the Lt. Col. boarded a train for Fort Devens, Mass., located approximately 50 miles from Boston.

It was early the next morning (0200 hrs) when we arrived at Ft. Devens, tired, feeling a bit gritty, but happy. My shipboard buddy from Bristol, Maine, decided to go to town and "slip" around. We visited the 1st "Bar & Grille" that had music & dancing. Two Waves, my buddy and I danced the morning away. Later in the afternoon, five GI's including myself, took a taxi for our trip to Boston. Thence, we each took a train or bus to our respective home towns.

After 31 days furlough our "orders" were to report to the Air Corps Replacement Depot and Rest Camp in Atlantic City, New Jersey. How lucky can one get?!?!

We were processed again, given back pay and billeted at one of the Hotels on the Boardwalk. I ventured out and found Pat, Tom, Burt Shilling and I believe, Carrington. We spent a few days together enjoying our fellowship until everyone was re-assigned to their respective bases. I believe the men were assigned to Grenier Fld., New Hampshire (the same base we flew out of when going overseas). I was sent to the Hospital for repairs. I ended up at the England General, on the Boardwalk, until January of '46. Thence to Bruns General in Santa Fe, New Mexico, then to Brooks General in Ft. Sam Houston, San Antonio, Texas.

On May 29, 1946 I was honorably discharged and sent home. As you can surmise, I spent 10 months recuperating and having various operations, and treatments for my "chronic sinusitis allergic rhinitus". I was informed that I should have been grounded and should not have been flying combat. The high altitudes raised havoc with my well being!!

Be that as it may, you have now learned the details of my departure from the 726th and how I spent my remaining days (1 yr) in the beloved Air Corps. I would not have changed a thing.

It seems, from what I learned through our discussions (Balzer & yourself), that the Crew was dismantled before you all had left Castallucio. Is this true?? Perhaps you can shed some light on this for me?? Please try and may I hear from you soon?

Kindest regards to you & Dorothy.

Sincerely,

Achi

Achi

p.s.   *The attached data are for your keeping. I designed the 451st patch & wings and had them made for an occasion just like this. I only wish we could have done it in person.*

November 30th 1999

Hello George,

Just a few lines to let you and Dorothy know that all is well with the Kozakis Clan.
The past six weeks came and went like a blink of an eye and I'm still trying to complete
the "addition" to the homestead! We are in the midst of a construction boom in the
Houston area and Contractors are hard to come by. Most of the heavy work is completed
and now begins the interior finishes, such as selecting colors, lighting fixtures and the like.
This is Rena's job. I just pay the bills!

Well old buddy, I'm sure you're getting plenty of rain in Philly this time of the year. We,
on the other hand, have been dry as a bone in a desert. Because of your wet weather, I'm
sure you're not out there walking around in the rain. Thus, I've gathered some excerpts
from the on going book I've been writing during the past few years and I'm enclosing them
for your perusal and I hope, enjoyment.

"Best Seat in the House" is the title of my book. Why this title? Well, I'll tell you! Flying
the Emerson Turret for thirty-five missions gives me this privilege and I'm speaking with
authority and experience. I'm sure you'll agree with me. The panoramic view, at times was
beautiful and breathtaking, especially when the weather was CAVU. On the other hand, it
was pretty frightening during a bomb run when the flak was so thick you walk on it!!

George, I still hear your voice over the intercom asking, "Kozakis, see any flak yet?"
I would come back, "not a thing" and then suddenly we would be jolted about like
pop corn caused by the flak tracking our aircraft. We cursed about it then, but laughing
about it now!

I've kept my combat experiences to myself in the past, but now I believe is the time to tell
my story. Especially when some of the younger generations don't' even know what
"D-Day" was. Sad, isn't it??

I recall one day we were sitting around in our tent and shooting the breeze about our crew.
A brief review follows:

H.S. Patterson, Pilot (28 years old). Hometown: Franklin, Indiana. Pat was like a big
brother to us. A great pilot and someone you could lean on. He, being the oldest
replacement pilot in the Squadron, made our lives safer because he wasn't cocky and
didn't make foolish mistakes, When we flew together, it was strictly business - everything
by the book. And when we weren't flying, he would always look out for our well being.

Thomas Thurman "Jug-Butt 3" (27 years old). Hometown: Crossville, Tennessee.

Tom was the appointed Squadron Gunnery Officer. He was notorious for suckering the boys in skeet shooting - making wagers. Tom would always win! His past time included selling clothes (civilian) that he received from his father's Haberdashery back in Tennessee.

Burton Shilling, Navigator (21 years old). Hometown: East Islip, Long Island, NY.
The quiet type, soft spoken and always very serous. His navigation skills were extremely accurate - always on course and on time. Burt became one of the Squadron's Lead Navigators.

William, Bill Bodie, Bombardier (22 years old). Hometown: Buffalo, NY. Bill was an easy going guy, lots of laughs in the nose of the aircraft. "Dead Eye" was his reputation and call number. Whenever we flew Lead ship, he most always made a "shack" (bulls eye)!!

George W. Really Jr., Flight Engineer & Top Turret Gunner, (21 years old). Hometown: Philadelphia, Penn. George did his job very well. One time, putting out a fire with his bare hands earned him the Soldier's Medal. George always bragged about the candy bars that were mad in Philly. He made his point - they were delicious!

Walter A. Carrington, Radio Operator & Waist Gunner (24 years old). Hometown: Waterburg, Connecticut. Walt was also a quiet type and kept to himself (except on payday) and wrote letters to his wife almost every day. He always set aside part of his pay to gamble at the N.C.O. club. It seems he managed to win most of the time!

Lauren A. Balzer, Armorer & Ball Turret Gunner (20 years old). Hometown: Portland, Oregon. Lauren would constantly "bitch" about a civilian who would complain because he would have to stand in the bus on his way to and from his defense job.
(A story about this guy was written in the *Yank* Magazine printed weekly) Lauren would always say that he'd swap places with that defense worker in a blink of an eye, without any bitching!

Achilles Kozakis, Nose Turret Gunner (21 years old). Hometown: Lynn, Massachusetts. First generation of Greek ancestry, sometimes affectionately known as "Greek". Achilles didn't smoke & he didn't drink! But he did love to listen to music whenever he could find it, dancing whenever he could find a partner and singing whenever the mood struck him. Let me add that Achilles liked the girls!!

Walter E. O'Laughlin, Waist Gunner (21 years old). Hometown: Monticello, Illinois. Walter had an Irish brogue as thick as Scottish kilts! O'Laughlin liked to gamble also, only he would almost always lose. This was his second tour of duty as waist gunner, a transfer form the Eighth Air Force. He was conscientious when it came to his work - a good man to have on our crew.

Last but not least -

Demetrio, Page Rodriguez Jr., Tail Turret Gunner (23 years old). Hometown: Taos, New Mexico. Page a good gunner and a better dice player. His game was chasing girls whenever he went into town. I must add, it was slim pickin's for Page around Foggia.

Quite a crew, huh? I'd say the <u>best</u> in the Squadron.

Well old buddy, it's time to knock it off for now. More *"Poop from Group"* to follow.

Take care of yourself and stay out of the rain. I hope you had a pleasant and thankful Thanksgiving Holiday. We had a full house!! My regards to Dorothy.

Sincerely,

Achi

Achi

p.s.   I have your photo on my desk and see you every day. Hoping some day we'll meet again. "You all" are a beautiful pair!!

Note: Taken by the Camera Gunner
from the right waiste position
on my 10th mission over
Linz, Austria.

THE **88**ᴍᴍ **FLAK**

TOO CLOSE FOR COMFORT
ONE EXPLODING, TWO
ON THIER WAY.

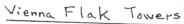

Vienna Flak Towers

Recreation Facilities (Parks)
are built around the Towers,
They are walled shut, bir.
are the only trespassers,
Photos taken by A. Kozakis
Oct. 1997.

Ploesti Refineries

S E C R E T

5-31-44   Plan Able

1st Attack Unit

1st Flight	2nd Flight	3rd Flight
SPECIAL MISSION - 804-Reed-Evans	LITTLE DUTCH P-25 - Mahon	B-090 -Morse
PATSY JACK B- 445-Threadgill	500 BOMBER K-234 Sparks	P-227-Brown
VERY GIRDEL I- 298-Prewitt	NICKLE PLATE CRATE X-876 -Fischer	I-568-Donahue
UNNAMED L-196 -Sprowls	J-219 -Thompson	C-754-Freeman
HOPE SCRATCH R- 209-Wodlund	856 -Paddock	G-178-Johnson
SUSAN DIANE M- 238-Pearson	A-140 -McQuuitt	E-426-McKelvy
	Spares - A-145-Anderson D-475-Cannon	
Start Engines - 0520   Taxi - 0530

2nd Attack Unit

1st Flight	2nd Flight	3rd Flight
O-250-Miller Capt Anderson	W-429-Small	E-808-Kearney
E-208-Kelly-Kaurauf	T-067-Bell	I-236-O'Connor
K-541-Hagen	A-082-Monson	P-114-Coyle
S-229-Sturman	H-530-McCutcheon	B-188-Johnson
R-580-Blair	D-256-Haun	E-276-McCollester
M-078-Moser	J-102-Pratt	L-757-Fulton
	Spares- Z-460-Hornbeck P-34 -Steinburg	
Start Engines - 0530   Taxi - 0540

TIMES: Take-off - 0540   Key Point - 0803 at 12000
Depart Base - 0640   ETA - 1319

RENDEZVOUS: 451st will rendezvous with 484 in rectangular course around
Bovino and Candola from 0640 to 0701

ESCORT: Penetration 48 P-38 0805 en route Mayflower 1
"   48 P-51 0950 4510N-2440E Mayflower 2
Target Cover: 48 P-38 0950 to 1040 target Mayflower 3
Withdrawal: 48 P-38 1105 4433N-2432E Mayflower 4

Target Information: Time - 1030   Altitude - 22,000
Axis - 180   Rally - Right

Communications:	Command 4085 Kcs	VHF - Able	
Call	Recall	Aldis	Flares
484th Greenherd 42	Paper	Red U Unit	Red-Red-Rendezvous
451st Greenherd 43	"	Red V Victor	Red-Red-Abandon Primary
461st Greenherd 41	"	Red W William	Red-Yellow-Climb
			Yellow-Yellow-Level Off
			Green-Yellow-Descend
			Green-Turn on I.P.

Squadron Colors: 724-White   725-Red   726-Green   727-Yellow   5.31

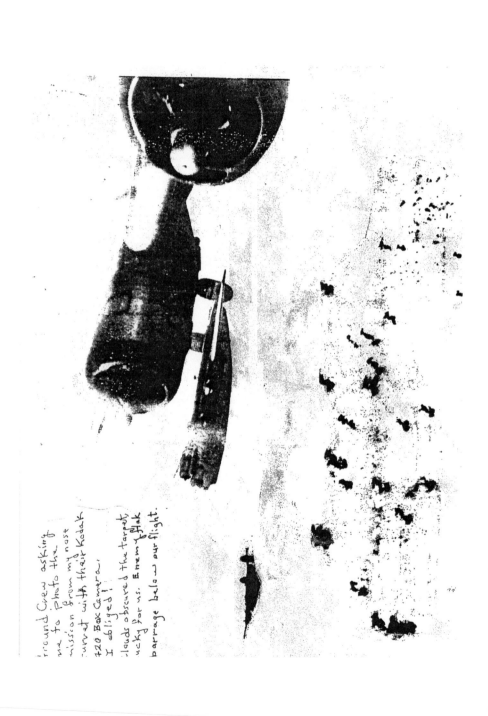

Ground Crew asking me to Photo the mission from my nose turret with their Kodak #20 Box Camera. I obliged! Clouds obscured the target ucky for us. Enemy flak barrage below our flight.

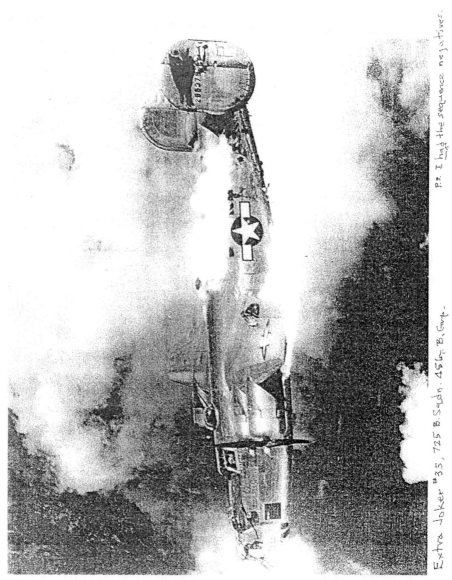

Extra Joker #35, 725 B. Sqdn. 456 B. Grp.

P: I had the sequence negatives.

B-24, "Extra Joker"

was shot down by enemy fighters while on a bombing mission over Markerslorf Airdrome near Vienna, Austria. Approximately six seconds elapsed between the snapping of the first photo and last photo. "Extra Joker" exploded seconds later. There were no survivors.

A hole in trailing edge of wing and beginning of a fire can be seen at the left wing root.

Heat buckling skin near left wing root. Fire can be seen erupting from small window & bottom of fuselage.

Fire has engulfed the fuselage and underside of left wing.

Over Vienna, a tail-end attack by a
German ME-109 fighter aircraft,
Extra Joker #35 is hit by a 20mm cann

Hit in the wing gas tanks, petrol gushing
out of aircraft.
Crew trying to evacuate aircraft.
(See gun turret positions.)

Aircraft ablaze leaves no time for
crew to evacuate. Next moment, plane goe
down in nose drive. Down, down, down.
All crew members: K.I.A.

Note: Crew has less than one minute to
evacuate before aircraft explodes.

Leo Stoutsenberger/Photo/Gunner
gave me the sequence negatives.
They were lost 50 years ago.

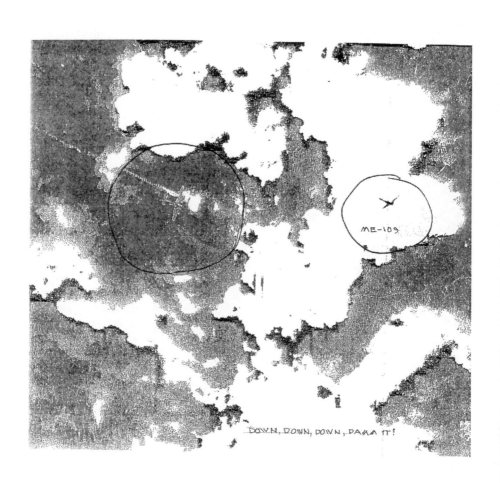

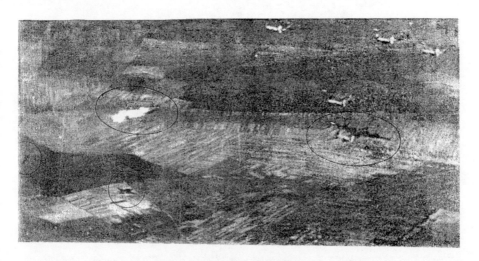

CHEWED UP BY FIGHTER AIRCRAFT (No Clouds To Hide In)

SMOKE POTS VEILING THE TARGET AREA

When oil became the primary target after D-Day, the Fifteenth drew the crude oil refineries around Ploesti, Budapest, and Vienna; *this red-tailed 451st Bomb Group Liberator was chewed by fighters over Austria.*

CROSSING THE ALPS - COMING AND GOING

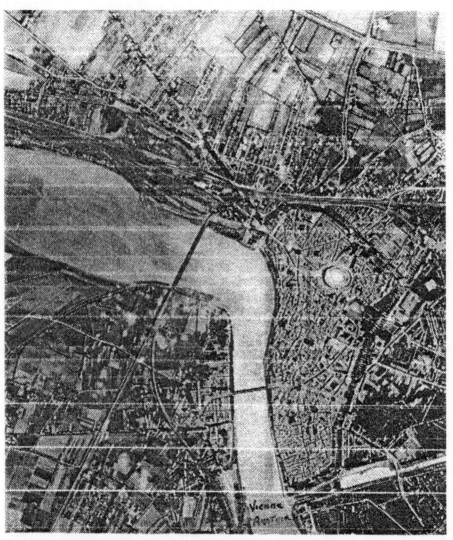

"The 'Big V' - Vienna, Austria"

Kate Did The Impossible Again But She Shudda Stood At Home

A 15TH AAF BASE, Italy, Dec. 19—"Ice Kold Katie," a 15th AAF Liberator bomber as old to combat as the song she's named after, did the impossible again Sunday, coming home after a mission to Germany after absorbing all the punishment four Kraut ME-109s could dish out. It was 1st Lt. Doyle M. Kizzire, Birmingham, Ala., who brought "Katie" home—"home" to the old gal being the service squadron where she has spent six of the 13 months in her combat career partially dissected and having her wounds repaired.

Engine trouble forced Lt. Boyle to drop out of a B-24 formation en route to Germany. Finally "Katie" snapped out of it, and was able to rejoin the formation just in time to drop her bombs. It was then that the MEs dropped by. Within a couple of minutes "Katie" was as beaten up and bedraggled as she was last February when she was jumped by a flock of enemy fighters over Regensburg. One fuel tank was pierced by a 20 mm. shell. Both rudders were riddled and one aileron shot up. Nobody volunteered to count the number of bullet holes in her thin skin.

So "Katie" is back "home" again. Someday, when she's in tiptop shape again, she may give it another try.

12/20/44 Pilot: Lt. Kizzire, Briefed for Brux- 10/10 cloud cover, Bombed Secondary Target, Linz Austria M.Y. (my 10th mission -17th sortie)
(P.S. They junked her for spare parts)

Photographie einer
deutschen Untergrund-Zeitung

Das Neue Deutschland

„Die Zukunft gehört jenen, die sich auf ...

Erscheint halbmonatlich   Süddeutsche Ausgabe

15. Januar 194..

Stoss in's Leere

Die Oberste Heeresleitung spielt ihre letzte Karte aus. An der Westfront versucht Rundstedt in verzweifelten Gegenstössen dem Gegner weit genug zurückzudrängen, um Luft für die letzte deutsche Verteidigungslinie...

Die Nachkriegspläne der NSDAP

Partei „Kernverbände" bereiten Vernichtung des ganzen Volkes vor

Wir haben heute Eines gemeinsam mit den Nazivorwort: Das Wissen, dass der Krieg unwiderbar verloren ist.

Während aber wir daraus die Schlussfolgerung ziehen, die allein den Weiterbestand Deutschlands und unseres Volkes sichern kann...

Soldatenbrief

Wir Soldaten wollen nichts von Politik hören, Vaterländische braucht man ebenso zu lehren und was die Bonzen zu Hause einreden...

Heimkehr der Vergeltungswaffe

Herr Goebbels und die verheerende Wirkung der V2 in England in das grösstes Fiasko geschrieben...

Krise in Japan

Künftige Generationen als Kriegsopfer

Edelweiss-Jugend

Fremdenverkehr im Dritten Reich

Betrug am deutschen Volke:

Hitlers Neujahrsrede gefälscht

Dem neuen Deutschland

Krieg, Handel und Piraterei

Kriegsgefangenenfürsorge

Soldaten!

CPSIA information can be obtained at www.ICGtesting.com
Printed in the USA
LVOW08s2009290316

481260LV00002BA/377/P

9 781465 369932